Understanding and Using
Scientific Evidence

Understanding and Using Scientific Evidence

How to Critically Evaluate Data

Richard Gott and Sandra Duggan

SAGE Publications
London • Thousand Oaks • New Delhi

© Richard Gott and Sandra Duggan 2003

First published 2003

Apart from any fair dealing for the purposes of research or private study, or criticism or review, as permitted under the Copyright, Designs and Patents Act, 1988, this publication may be reproduced, stored or transmitted in any form, or by any means, only with the prior permission in writing of the publishers, or in the case of reprographic reproduction, in accordance with the terms of licences issued by the Copyright Licensing Agency. Inquiries concerning reproduction outside those terms should be sent to the publishers.

 SAGE Publications
6 Bonhill Street
London EC2A 4PU

SAGE Publications Inc
2455 Teller Road
Thousand Oaks, California 91320

SAGE Publications India Pvt Ltd
B-42 Panchsheel Enclave
Post Box 4109
New Delhi 100 017

Library of Congress Control Number: 2002110569

A catalogue record for this book is available from the British Library

ISBN 0 7619 7083 5
ISBN 0 7619 7084 3 (pbk)

Typeset by Dorwyn Ltd, Rowlands Castle, Hants.
Printed in Great Britain by Athenaeum Press, Gateshead

Contents

Acknowledgements

Every effort has been made to trace the copyright holders but if any have been inadvertently overlooked the publishers will be pleased to make the necessary arrangements at the first opportunity.

Chapter 1

Introduction

Introduction

Here are some recent science-related headlines:

Hidden significance of a man's ring finger The longer a man's fingers are relative to his height, the more likely he is to suffer from depression	*Meningitis vaccine cuts cases by up to 85%*	*A close brush with poison* Toothpaste can contain amounts of fluoride damaging to adults and lethal to children. Yet manufacturers are lax about providing warnings or directions about a substance that is almost as toxic as arsenic

What do you need to know to make up your mind whether you believe these headlines or not or to challenge the experts? To make an informed decision, you need:

- some understanding of the subject matter (e.g. of depression, vaccination or the effect of fluoride); and
- an understanding of what makes 'good' scientific evidence.

1.1 What is the book about?

This book is about the second of these: the understanding needed to explore scientific evidence thoroughly. Our aim is to take the reader through some of the basic ideas which underlie any piece of evidence. We hope that, by the end of the book, you will know how to get 'inside' the evidence to make an informed decision as to whether or not the evidence is trustworthy and, if so, how much reliance can be placed on it.

3

The book can be used as a 'dip-in' resource or a background reader. We will cover a lot of difficult ideas, but also some very simple ones which are included for completeness and for the relative newcomer to experimental work in science. For those with a good science background, a skim through the topics and the text will soon identify the important sections.

All of the ideas in the book will not apply to every piece of evidence. In much of ecology, for instance, ideas like measurement error may not be relevant but an understanding of sampling may be critical. Conversely, in chemistry and physics in school science, sampling is often not an issue.

The book is not about scientific 'method'. Science evolves in all kinds of ways: there is no one fixed method. But whatever method is adopted, the evidence plays a crucial role whether it be to test out theory, as a basis for prediction or, as in industry, as a means of reporting quality. We also make no attempt to cover philosophical aspects of the nature of science and scientific reasoning but refer the reader to some of the many excellent texts on these issues.[1] Our main concern here is with scientific evidence grounded in data, although in the last chapter we acknowledge briefly the influence of other factors on the evaluation of, and the decision-making that results from, the evidence.

1.2 Who is this book for?

This book is for anybody who wants to know how to understand and evaluate scientific data including

- Those who want to deepen their understanding of scientific evidence whether in relation to issues involving science in everyday life, in the press, the media or in scientific papers.
- 'New' researchers in psychology and social science as well as those in physical and biological science, wherever research methods is a part of the course.
- Students on introductory university courses where an understanding of experimental data is required.
- Students on sixth form courses in science, psychology and social science as well as some of the 'newer' courses such as AS level in public understanding of science or courses in media science.

---

[1] For example:
Chalmers, A.F. (1978) *What is This Thing Called Science?* OUP;
Dunbar, R. (1995) *The Trouble With Science.* Faber and Faber, London;
Giere, R.N. (1979) *Understanding Scientific Reasoning.* Holt Rinehart and Winston;
Wolpert, L. (1992) *The Unnatural Nature of Science.* Faber and Faber.

- Trainee science teachers both in relation to their teaching and in relation to educational research.
- Practising science teachers.

The book can be used for the evaluation of any scientific evidence from research papers to the data increasingly becoming available on the Internet. It can also serve as a useful manual for the investigator while carrying out any sort of practical work.

The aim of the book is to get beyond the ritual doing of practical work or the routine analysis of data into an understanding of the ideas that underpin both the successful experimenter and the critical evaluator.

1.3 Why does understanding evidence matter?

We are constantly confronted by evidence in our everyday lives. Some of it may not affect us too directly and we can therefore decide to ignore it or duck the issue. Many people, for example, have responded to the BSE (bovine spongiform encephalitis) issue by saying 'it's too late – I've eaten beef all my life' or have just ignored it hoping that the problem will go away. But nearly all of us have to make some decisions where the evidence is, or should be, paramount, such as choosing which method of birth control to use for instance. We may of course rely on 'experts' or trusted friends for advice but we cannot then blame them if things go wrong – we should be able make our own decisions based on the best available evidence. In the case of birth control there is plenty of readily available evidence to examine. On other issues, such as BSE, the evidence may be hard to find or, in some aspects, non-existent. But we need to be clear about this. In any issue involving science we should ask:

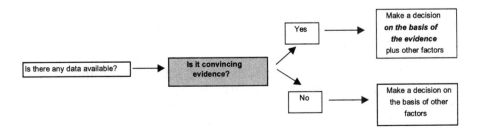

Where there is no convincing evidence one way or another, then we make a decision as best we can based on factors such as cost, status

of the individuals who are trying to persuade us, or simply a gut reaction!

1.4 How is evidence used?

There are three main ways in which scientific evidence is used: to look for a *link*, a *difference* or a *change*.

1. *A link*: Data can be used as evidence to demonstrate the strength of a link, relationship or association in various ways. The strongest link is a direct association or one of *cause and effect*. In its simplest form, if I change X, then Y will happen. A simple example is the relationship between mass and the stretch of a rubber band. This sort of direct relationship can be used to predict behaviour: if you know the relationship between mass and the stretch of a rubber band, you can predict what will happen if you attach a known mass to the rubber band, within limits.

2. *A difference*: Data can also be used as evidence to decide whether two or more groups differ significantly from each another. For example, 'Is there a significant difference in outcomes between the treatment of cancer in area X compared to area Y?' By gathering information on the two samples, and applying appropriate statistics, we will be able to establish the probability (or chance) of whether or not the two outcomes really are different.

3. *A change*: Data can also be used as evidence to establish change with time: we might want to find out how the vitamin content of a type of apple changes between the time of picking and the sell-by date. Again by gathering data and using appropriate statistics we can provide evidence to answer the question.

1.5 Assessing the evidence: validity and reliability

Before we launch into the details, let us first of all emphasise the importance of two fundamental ideas, those of validity and reliability. Put crudely they mean 'did the experiment answer the question satisfactorily?' (validity), and as a necessary condition of that, 'was the data reliable – could somebody else do it all again and get the same answer, or was it such a poorly designed experiment that the results were random and meaningless?' (reliability). These ideas need to be at the back of your mind whenever you design your own experiment, or attempt to make sense of the results of one done by others. Science positively requires that we are brutally sceptical about its evidence; only by being critical can we be sure that we are not misleading ourselves.

1.5.1 Validity

Validity means:

Does the evidence really provide the answer to the question?

So when you are considering the validity of any piece of science, you need to examine the design of the experiment or investigation, the measurement, the way the results are presented, the interpretation of the results and the conclusion, i.e. the whole thing. The evidence might provide the answer to another question, not the one it claims to. If an instrument designed to measure performance-enhancing drugs in the blood is affected by some other constituent, a soft drink perhaps, then the measurement you have taken is invalid.

1.5.2 Reliability

Reliability means:

Can you trust the measurements?

So when you are considering reliability, you need to be convinced that if you measured the same thing with the same instrument on a number of occasions you would arrive at the same value. Some of the questions you might ask to explore the reliability of measurements are:

- was the instrument good enough to take those measurements?
- is the range of repeated measurements reported?
- are the conditions under which the measurements were taken described? etc.

1.5.3 Validity and reliability – a one-way relationship

If you think about validity and reliability, can you see that an experiment might be invalid but still be reliable? Supposing you measure the distance that toy cars of different weights travel down a ramp – you test each car lots of times and with very accurate measurement. Your results are reliable. But you conclude that the heavier toy cars go faster. You have not measured time, so you cannot talk about speed – your conclusion is invalid. All you can conclude is that heavier toy cars go further.

But although an investigation can be invalid but still reliable, it cannot be unreliable and valid. If it is unreliable then it is always invalid because the measurements cannot be trusted and therefore the interpretation of the results and the conclusion cannot be trusted:

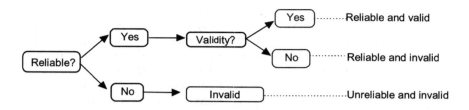

Another way of looking at the relationship between validity and reliability is to think of validity including reliability:

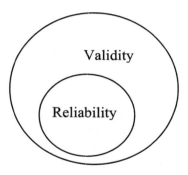

1.6 Looking forward and looking back

To believe evidence or be convinced by data in science you need to LOOK FORWARD and LOOK BACK.

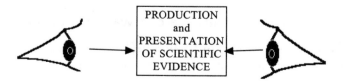

The goal in 'looking forward' is to produce valid and reliable evidence and you must keep that goal in mind all the time right from the very first design stages, through the measurement stages and especially when you are writing up your report. The idea is that anyone else could look at your evidence and see that it is valid and reliable. So while you are looking forward, you must keep in mind that eventually you and other people will be 'looking back' at your work – that is evidence.

By understanding all the processes involved in 'looking forward' to arriving at valid and reliable scientific evidence (or evidence that we can trust or attach some weight to), we can then look at other people's evidence, e.g. in the press or journals, and 'look back'. But you cannot simply learn these processes one by one because you need to understand how they make up the whole.

1.7 The structure of the book

The following flowchart (p. 10) shows the structure of the book. The arrows suggest some ways you might choose to use it.

If you want to get an idea of basic experimental design then you might read chapters 2, 3, 5, 6 and 7. If you want to know about more complex designs you would be wise to read Chapter 4 too. If you are interested in using, analysing and interpreting large amounts of data, then chapters 8 and 9 address these issues. The flowchart is reproduced at the beginning of each chapter to help you navigate your own path.

1.8 How to use this book

You will soon notice that the text is not continuous. Periodically you are asked to pause and answer some questions. These places in the text are indicated by

☆ ☆ ☆ ☆ ☆ ☆

The questions are designed to make sure that you have understood the previous section so that you are confident to move on to the next. The questions are based in a wide range of contexts – in the three scientific disciplines (physics, chemistry and biology) and in everyday contexts. This is because we hope that:

1. readers interested in particular scientific disciplines will engage with an example in that discipline and also see how the principle applies to other disciplines;
2. the reader will deepen his/her understanding by applying the principle to everyday issues;

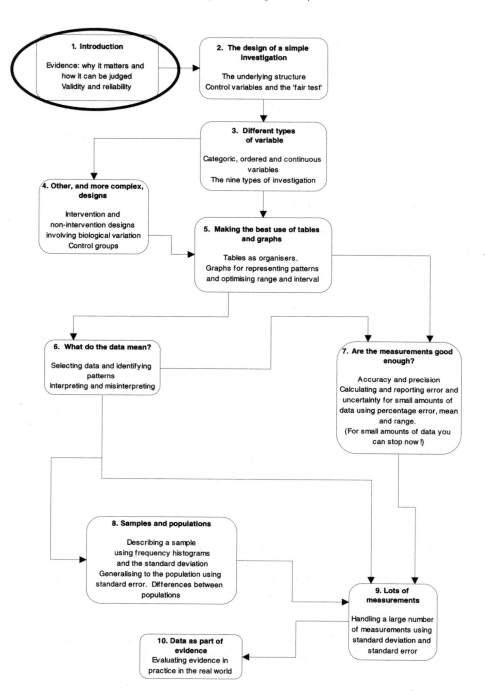

1. Introduction

Evidence: why it matters and how it can be judged
Validity and reliability

2. The design of a simple investigation

The underlying structure
Control variables and the 'fair test'

3. Different types of variable

Categoric, ordered and continuous variables
The nine types of investigation

4. Other, and more complex, designs

Intervention and non-intervention designs involving biological variation
Control groups

5. Making the best use of tables and graphs

Tables as organisers.
Graphs for representing patterns and optimising range and interval

6. What do the data mean?

Selecting data and identifying patterns
Interpreting and misinterpreting

7. Are the measurements good enough?

Accuracy and precision
Calculating and reporting error and uncertainty for small amounts of data using percentage error, mean and range.
(For small amounts of data you can stop now !)

8. Samples and populations

Describing a sample using frequency histograms and the standard deviation
Generalising to the population using standard error. Differences between populations

9. Lots of measurements

Handling a large number of measurements using standard deviation and standard error

10. Data as part of evidence
Evaluating evidence in practice in the real world

3. readers who are involved in education will recognise possible ways of teaching the principles in the context of school/college science.

Throughout the book we have used very simple science so as not to complicate the ideas. Some, but by no means all, of the examples are familiar school investigations. The reader should also note that we have used the terms experiment and investigation somewhat interchangeably although we are aware that in school science, 'investigation' is usually taken to mean open ended experiments. The ideas in this book apply to all kinds of practical work from routine measurements to standard experiments to more open ended practical work. Having said that, the more open ended the task and the more it involves problem-solving rather than guided instruction, the more the ideas in this book will be needed.

For maximum effect, the reader is advised to try relating the ideas to topical issues in the press or on the television. Discussion is also an excellent, and probably the best, way of developing understanding.

1.9 A note on how the book can be used in teacher education

For students on teacher training courses, a glance at the headings in the book will reveal a strong link to elements of the National Curriculum and the examination syllabi for GCSE and A level courses in all the sciences.

More specifically, for *primary* teachers the book addresses the need for trainees to understand the basic principles of experimental science identified by the Teacher Training Agency for Initial Teacher Training:

'Trainees must demonstrate that they know and understand the processes of planning, carrying out and evaluating scientific investigations including e.g.

- the nature of variables including: identification of categoric, independent and dependent variables, and recognition of discrete and continuous variables;
- the structure and use of controlled experiments, taking into account all the relevant variables to allow a valid comparison of different sets of data;
- the ways in which samples can be selected, how this will influence the outcomes of investigation and how this can be

recognised when findings are interpreted;
- the need to plan investigations so as to use the most appropriate scientific methods for the collection, analysis and interpretation of evidence;
- possible reasons for experimental findings not supporting accepted scientific evidence, including: extent of available evidence, natural variation in measurements, limitations of resources and experimental design;
- the fact that outcomes of an investigation should be considered in the light of the original question and the wider body of available and relevant scientific evidence.'[2]

For *secondary* science teachers, the book addresses the knowledge and understanding required 'to teach scientific skills and methods explicitly' and ensure that pupils make progress in their use, including how to:

- ensure that pupils know how to use them safely, correctly and appropriately in their science work, including teaching the appropriate use of instruments to increase pupils' accuracy in observation and measurement;
- design experiments and investigations so that they are likely to yield sufficient reliable evidence to enable pupils to explain these in terms of scientific knowledge and understanding;
- teach pupils to identify relevant variables in different contexts;
- teach pupils to judge the range of observations and measurements they need to make, when and why these need to be repeated, and how to deal with anomalous or discrepant results;
- teach pupils to examine evidence for validity and reliability by considering questions of accuracy, error and discrepancy;
- teach pupils to identify increasingly quantitative patterns and relationships when appropriate;
- teach pupils to draw conclusions and to relate these to underlying scientific ideas;
- teach pupils to use information technology for more effective collection, analysis and presentation of data, *e.g. data logging; producing graphs from spreadsheets*;
- consider with pupils, where necessary, the reasons why the outcomes of a particular activity do not demonstrate what was intended, *e.g. because of faulty equipment, poor experimental design or poor technique*.'[3]

---

[2] ITT National Curriculum for primary science. Annex E in 'Circular 4/98 Requirements for ITT', TTA, London.
[3] ITT National Curriculum for secondary science. Annex H in 'Circular 4/98 Requirements for ITT', TTA, London.

In addition, the TTA requires physics trainees to understand 'basic statistical techniques for processing data and estimating errors' and biology teachers to know 'basic statistical theory relating to distributions and sampling'. All secondary science teachers are required to teach numerical awareness in terms of an 'appropriate degree of precision'. These issues are explored in the book.

Where are you?

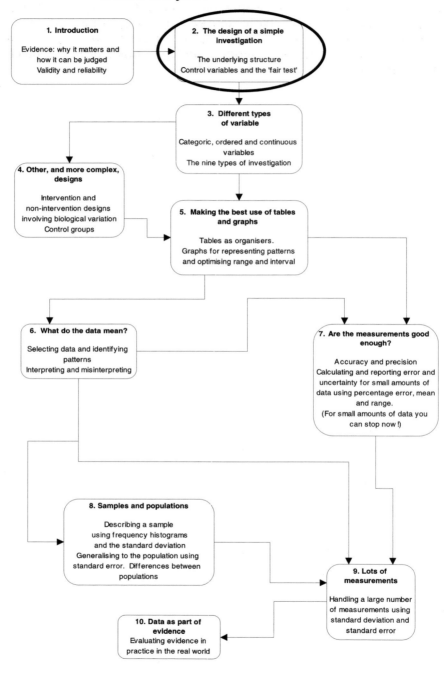

1. Introduction

Evidence: why it matters and
how it can be judged
Validity and reliability

**2. The design of a simple
investigation**

The underlying structure
Control variables and the 'fair test'

**3. Different types
of variable**

Categoric, ordered and continuous
variables
The nine types of investigation

**4. Other, and more complex,
designs**

Intervention and
non-intervention designs
involving biological variation
Control groups

**5. Making the best use of tables
and graphs**

Tables as organisers.
Graphs for representing patterns
and optimising range and interval

6. What do the data mean?

Selecting data and identifying
patterns
Interpreting and misinterpreting

**7. Are the measurements good
enough?**

Accuracy and precision
Calculating and reporting error and
uncertainty for small amounts of
data using percentage error, mean
and range.
(For small amounts of data you
can stop now !)

8. Samples and populations

Describing a sample
using frequency histograms
and the standard deviation
Generalising to the population using
standard error. Differences between
populations

**9. Lots of
measurements**

Handling a large number
of measurements using
standard deviation and
standard error

**10. Data as part of
evidence**
Evaluating evidence in
practice in the real world

Chapter 2

The design of a simple investigation

Introduction

Government backs fluoride for all

Trendy ice cream has more dioxin than refinery effluent

New drug will boost breast cancer fight

When you see headlines like those above, how do you know whether to trust them? How do we know that fluoride is a really 'good idea', that the 'trendy' ice cream really has more dioxin, or that the new drug for breast cancer is effective? One of the first things that will help you to judge whether or not a headline like this is valid is to look in the article for the *structure* of the design of the experiment that lies behind the claim and then decide whether the structure itself is valid.

To do this, we need to understand the basic principles which underlie the structure of the design of an experiment or investigation. Then we can decide whether or not the design is such that it will be able to answer the question. Remember that this understanding of basic principles is useful in planning an experiment or investigation ourselves (looking forward) or in evaluating somebody else's work or a report in the press.

Is the structure of the design valid?

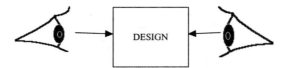

We shall start with the simplest design but one which underlies many scientific experiments.

2.1 The underlying structure

We saw in the last chapter, that the purpose of collecting evidence is to explore the strength of a link or connection of some kind, or a difference, or a change over time. Any of these imply (see the examples) that there are at least two factors to consider and that these factors can change. We can call these factors 'variables' – a variable simply means something that can *change* or *vary*. The design of an experiment or investigation is about looking for some kind of link between two (or more) variables.

2.1.1 Looking for links

The key variables
Suppose a scientist wants to find out what affects how quickly water boils in a kettle, which is the sort of thing a kettle manufacturer needs to know. The first step must be to make a list of all the variables that you suspect might influence the time for the water to boil. Here are some:

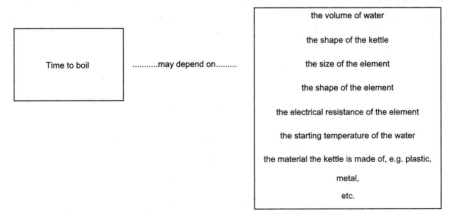

Let us now put all these variables in a circle, with the 'time to boil' in the middle.

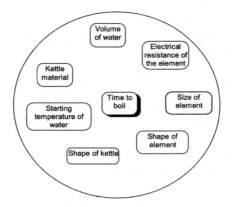

The variable at the centre of this circle is our main concern: we are trying to find out what makes this (*the time to boil*) vary. We predict/suspect that the time to boil will *depend* on one or more of the other variables. So the time to boil is called the DEPENDENT variable. We can then link the dependent variable to any of the other variables and create a question which can be tested. For example:

* How does *the shape of the kettle* affect the time to boil?
* How does *the electrical resistance of the element* affect the time to boil?

So we have arrived at two variables which form the underlying structure of our experiment. We have formulated a question which allows us to look for a link. In this case, the time to boil is our dependent variable. The other factor that we have chosen so that we can investigate its effect on the dependent variable is known as the INDEPENDENT variable – because we have *chosen* it ourselves, or chosen it *independently*.

Let's choose *the shape of the element* as our independent variable and link it to the dependent variable, *time to boil*, with an arrow:

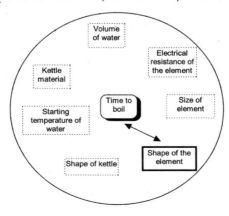

An experiment or investigation, in any branch of science, attempts to establish a link between an *independent* and a *dependent* variable:

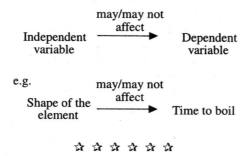

☆ ☆ ☆ ☆ ☆ ☆

Before you read on, can you identify the independent and dependent variable in the following?

First here are three school-type experiments in physics, chemistry and biology:

1. How does the mass of a pendulum affect the span of its 'swing'?
2. Investigate the factors that affect the rate of a chemical reaction.
3. Does moss grow better in (a) light or dark or (b) dry or moist conditions?

And here are two 'everyday' examples:

1. How is reaction time affected by alcohol intake?
2. Find out which of two reading methods is best for teaching children to read.[1]

Then look back to the three headlines and see if you can suggest the structure of an experiment lying behind the headlines.

1. 'Government backs fluoride for all'
2. 'Trendy ice cream has more dioxin than refinery effluent'
3. 'New drug will boost breast cancer fight'

☆ ☆ ☆ ☆ ☆ ☆

In the school examples, the independent variables are: (1) mass of the pendulum (2) the factors (e.g. temperature, particle size, etc.); (3) the conditions, namely light/dark or dry/moist. The dependent variables

---

[1] You may notice here that this example is fraught with difficulties in a way that the previous example is not. For instance, what do we define as a good reader? Will that be linked to clarity and diction or understanding? Investigating human behaviour is a very complex and difficult affair!

are the span of the swing, the rate of reaction and moss growth. In the everyday examples, the independent variables are alcohol intake and the reading methods. The dependent variables are the reaction time and some measure of reading ability.

You probably found you had to think harder about the headlines. In the first one, you might expect the investigators to have compared the beneficial effects of fluoride with that of not taking fluoride. So the independent variable is amount of fluoride (some unspecified amount and none) and the dependent variable is some measure of the beneficial effects (e.g. dental health). In the second and third headlines, the independent variables are type of chemical (ice cream or effluent) and type of drug (new and old drug), and the dependent variables are quantity of dioxin and some measure of breast cancer.

☆ ☆ ☆ ☆ ☆ ☆

2.2 The control variables and the 'fair test'

Once you have defined the question as revolving around these two key variables (the independent and dependent variables), the next decision concerns what to do with the rest of the variables in the circle.

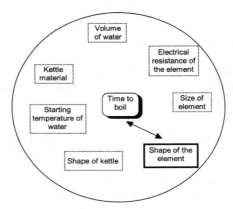

The answer is, wherever possible, to keep all the other variables the same or constant. And so our question becomes:

> How does the boiling time of the water depend on the shape of the element for jug-type kettles made of plastic with the same size element rated at 3kw (the electrical resistance) with 1 litre of water at a starting temperature of 8°C ... and so on.

Here we have kept the following variables the same:

- the volume of the water;
- the electrical resistance of the element;
- the size of the element;
- the shape of the kettle;
- the starting temperature of the water; and
- the kettle material.

In fact, as you will see, these are all the other variables in the circle which are outlined with a dotted line. These variables are usually called CONTROL variables to indicate that they must be kept under control. If we let them change in a haphazard way, then any results we get may be useless. For instance, imagine measuring the boiling time for a litre of water in a round metal kettle and then measuring how long a litre of water takes to boil in a plastic jug-type kettle. Clearly it is not 'fair' to make this comparison – both the shape *and* the material of the two kettles are different – so we will not know by how much each variable has influenced the boiling time. (Of course, if the question were just 'which kettle is best?', then it would be perfectly sensible, but that is not the question we posed earlier.) If possible, it is much simpler to change one variable at a time because then you are more likely to arrive at a clear conclusion.

When you design an experiment so that the relevant variables *are* controlled this is often referred to as a 'FAIR TEST'. A fair test has the following basic design:

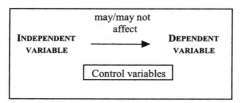

The fair test structure

Such a tightly defined question, of course, can be followed up by others, each of which looks at the effect of one of the other variables, for example, the shape of the kettle, this time keeping the shape of the element the same; or the material the kettle is made of – keeping the shape of the kettle and the shape of the element the same; and so on. Any one of these questions can be tested by designing a fair test in which the relevant variables are controlled.

2.2.1 Recognising the variables that might matter

We should note here that in looking for possible links and in selecting the relevant variables to control we are, consciously or unconsciously, using our knowledge of what is *likely* to be influencing the dependent variable. In this example, we are probably applying knowledge of physics of, for example, how the shape of the kettle might affect the boiling time, to the problem. We may exclude some variables such as room temperature in the above example, because we believe that they are not going to affect matters significantly. Ideally all variables should be considered and, if they are not controlled, then they should still be acknowledged. For example, we could state that, although temperature was not controlled, the kettle experiments were done within a range of room temperature X – Y °C. The same applies to humidity, air movement and so on.

So, because choosing the relevant variables depends on prior knowledge which can, of course, sometimes be wrong, there can be an element of unintentional 'bias' in choosing the 'relevant' variables. To avoid this sort of bias, in constructing the design you need to keep a very open mind as to what possible variables might affect the dependent variable. This is particularly applicable in investigations into human behaviour. Consider the following:

Does watching violent videos cause violent behaviour in
children?

Put violent behaviour in the middle of your variables circle and see how many factors you can think of that might influence violent behaviour in children. Your circle should be quite crowded! (You would also need to worry as to whether any connection was causal – it could be that some other factor – abuse perhaps – causes both the video watching *and* the violent behaviour!)

Another way of recognising the relevant variables, although with hindsight, is by looking carefully at the results themselves. If an expected pattern (association or difference) is not seen, then it may be because a relevant variable has not been controlled. If it is in your own investigation, then you may be able to go back and do the investigation again, this time controlling the 'forgotten' variable. If it is somebody else's work, then look hard to see whether they have stated that they have controlled all the variables that you think are relevant: they may not have.

☆ ☆ ☆ ☆ ☆ ☆

To make sure you understand the structure of the fair test, try drawing variable circles for two of the five investigations we looked at earlier. Identify the control variables:

1. How does the mass of a pendulum affect the time of its 'swing'?
2. Investigate the factors that affect the rate of a chemical reaction.
3. Does moss grow better in (a) light or dark and (b) dry or moist conditions?
4. How is reaction time affected by alcohol intake?
5. Find out which of two reading methods is best for teaching children to read.

☆ ☆ ☆ ☆ ☆ ☆

There are of course a lot of possible control variables of which we shall identify a few examples. In the first experiment, the length of the string and the starting position should be controlled. In the second, if the independent variable is temperature, then the control variables would include the type of chemical and the rate of stirring. In the moss investigation, the same species of moss should be used in the different conditions and, assuming that this is a laboratory experiment, the different containers should all be treated in the same way, e.g. exposure to occasional draughts or movement.

Again you will probably find that thinking about the control variables in the two everyday examples is more difficult. In the alcohol intake experiment, volunteers might be tested after increasing amounts of alcohol. In this case, the control variables would include the age and sex of the volunteers, the time between drinking and testing, the test itself and so on. The last example would include control variables such as the age and ability of the children and the teacher. Ideally, the children's previous experience both in and outside school should be controlled, but this is obviously difficult to do in practice. Control variables like this, which should be controlled but simply cannot be, will give rise to an increased uncertainty in our results – we shall look more carefully at this in Chapter 4.

☆ ☆ ☆ ☆ ☆ ☆

2.3 Looking forward and looking back again

Now that you can identify the underlying structure of a scientific experiment then you will see why the design matters for the *validity* of the whole experiment. (Remember, validity means 'Does the evidence really provide the answer to the question?')

> Validity requires that the correct independent and dependent variables are chosen and that other relevant variables are controlled. This constitutes a fair test.

If, in the design of an experiment, the wrong independent or dependent variable is chosen, then the results will be invalid no matter how well the measurements were taken or how well the results are presented. This may seem obvious but in reality it is not uncommon. Consider this example:

Lead in your tea?

A company selling packaged tea was concerned about the level of lead in their tea because the law states a maximum ($5mg\ kg^{-1}$). Ten samples of tea leaves were taken and a wide variation in the lead content was found. The scientists thought that the variation might be because the leaves were of different sizes and there was also some tea dust in the samples, the amount of which could vary between samples. So the leaves were sieved with two different mesh sizes resulting in

whole leaves   broken leaves   tea dust.

They then analysed the lead content in the whole leaves and in the tea dust. The lead content of the dust was much greater than in the whole leaves. They reported their results to the scientific director, suggesting that by reducing the amount of tea dust they could reduce the amount of lead in the packaged tea. The scientific director was not pleased – he said the results were *invalid*. Why? What mattered, he said, was the amount of lead in the tea infusion not the lead in the leaves. So he sent them back to try again. They had picked the wrong *dependent* variable. Instead of the tea leaves they should have been analysing the infusion made from the tea leaves. They had been trying to answer the wrong question.

Another reason why results are sometimes invalid is because all the relevant control variables have not been taken into account. Here is an example:

A botanist had been asked to determine the best type of soil composition for the growth of a plant which is the sole food supply of a rare butterfly. She set up some test beds of plants in a temperature-controlled greenhouse with five different soil compositions and carefully gave the plants the same amount of water each day. She checked their growth twice a day, measuring the height, the number of new leaves and recording the appearance of all the plants. But she did not notice that two of the five test beds were in the shade for a large part of the day. The results were therefore *invalid* because it was not possible to tell whether the poor growth of some plants was due to the soil composition or the lack of light. She had omitted to control the amount of light.

So when you are 'looking forward' and constructing your design, make sure you have the underlying structure clearly in your mind and make sure that your design will allow you to answer the question. And when you are 'looking back', you need to ask: Did the investigators select the correct variables (the independent, dependent and control variables) to answer the question?'

Another way of thinking about this, which we shall build on throughout the book, is as a 'decision tree'. The complete decision tree will act as a reminder of things to look out for in producing and examining scientific evidence. Below, is an example of how we might include the ideas we have introduced so far into a decision tree. But you should construct your own decision tree, in your own way. (It is best to put this at the top of a new sheet of paper so that you can add new ideas underneath, as you go through the book.)

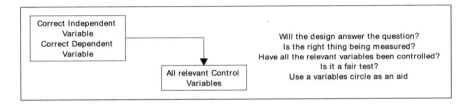

Notice that both the decision points so far concern structure and, hence, validity.

2.4 A note on the terminology

It is easy to confuse the terms 'variable', 'independent', 'dependent' and 'control' variables. We are going to use these terms here but there are alternatives that you might come across:

- The independent variable is sometimes called the 'input' variable.
- The dependent variable can be called the 'output' variable.
- Control variables are sometimes called 'fixed' variables or 'constants'.

Whatever you call them, the important idea is the underlying structure.

How does the [dependent/output] variable depend on the [independent/input] variable when the relevant [control/fixed/constant] variables are kept the same, so that the test is fair?

2.5 Other types of design

The above example is the simplest experimental design – it is sometimes called a 'clean' or a 'tight' design because it is the most
straightforward both to design and also, as we shall see later, to interpret. But this kind of design is not always

- appropriate; or
- possible.

There is, as we have noted in passing during this chapter and elsewhere, a very significant difference between scientific experiments and
those concerning educational issues or other issues concerning human
behaviour. For a science investigation, it is usually possible to assign
causation, or at least to have a good idea as to what might be causal
factors. Similarly measurements tend to be straightforward conceptually, even if sometimes very different technically.

In education or behavioural research on the other hand:

- it is often not possible to assign causation. For example, are violent
  behaviour and watching violent videos linked causally to each other
  or to a third factor? Or even a multiplicity of factors of nature and
  nurture origins?
- measurement is quite often easy technically – a questionnaire or
  interview – but very difficult and controversial conceptually. For
  example, what do we mean by 'violent behaviour'?

These, and other factors, make the notion of a 'simple scientific'
experiment in behavioural science less straightforward. Nevertheless
the basic structure is not a bad starting point and it can help to clarify
thinking about a complex issue. We shall look at some other and more
complex types of designs in Chapter 4.

2.6 Summary

- Any phenomena we wish to investigate will have a number of influ-
  ential factors associated with it.
- These factors, variables, have to be identified.
- These variables can be shown in a 'circle of variables' (see over page).
- Questions can be asked about the phenomena by linking two of
  these variables.
- One must be identified as the *independent* variable – the factor you
  want to find the effect *of*.

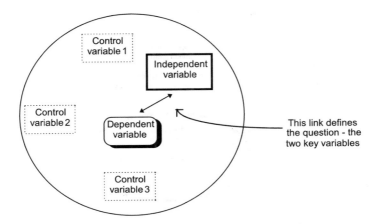

- The other must be identified as the *dependent* variable – the factor you want to find the effect *on*, the one you measure in relation to the independent variable.
- All the other variables must be taken into account by, if possible, keeping them constant throughout the experiment (the *control* variables). If this is not done then any results may, at best, be of limited use in pointing to what might be done next.
- The validity of the design depends on the construction of a *fair test*.

Look in the press for headlines or issues which involve science (like the ones below) and see if you can work out what the key variables would be to provide a valid experimental design for each issue.

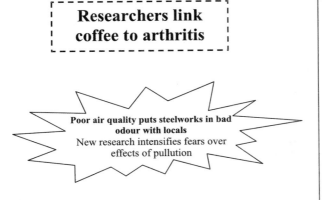

Vanilla dulls sweet craving
After nicotine patches for people who want to quit smoking come vanilla patches for chocolate addicts who want to lose weight. A study at St George's hospital in Tooting, south London, has found that vanilla-scented patches can significantly reduce the appetite for chocolate, sweet foods and drinks.

Where are you?

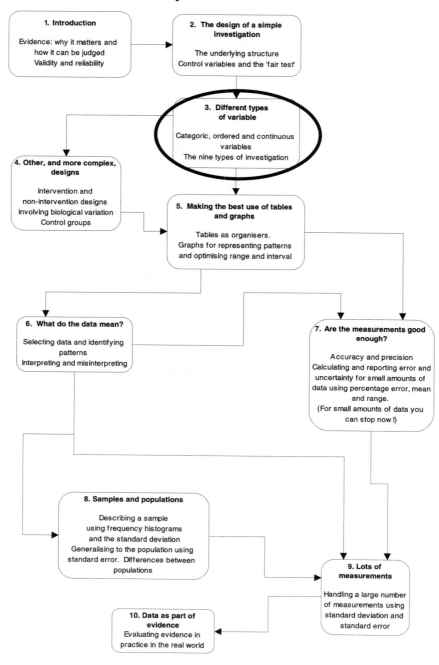

1. Introduction

Evidence: why it matters and how it can be judged
Validity and reliability

2. The design of a simple investigation

The underlying structure
Control variables and the 'fair test'

3. Different types of variable

Categoric, ordered and continuous variables
The nine types of investigation

4. Other, and more complex, designs

Intervention and non-intervention designs involving biological variation
Control groups

5. Making the best use of tables and graphs

Tables as organisers.
Graphs for representing patterns and optimising range and interval

6. What do the data mean?

Selecting data and identifying patterns
Interpreting and misinterpreting

7. Are the measurements good enough?

Accuracy and precision
Calculating and reporting error and uncertainty for small amounts of data using percentage error, mean and range.
(For small amounts of data you can stop now !)

8. Samples and populations

Describing a sample using frequency histograms and the standard deviation
Generalising to the population using standard error. Differences between populations

9. Lots of measurements

Handling a large number of measurements using standard deviation and standard error

10. Data as part of evidence
Evaluating evidence in practice in the real world

Chapter 3
Different types of variables

Introduction

```
┌ ─ ─ ─ ─ ─ ─ ─ ─ ─ ─ ─ ─ ┐
│   Researchers link      │
│   coffee to arthritis   │
└ ─ ─ ─ ─ ─ ─ ─ ─ ─ ─ ─ ─ ┘
```

**Poor air quality puts steelworks in bad
odour with locals**
New research intensifies fears over effects of
pollution

In the last chapter, we explored the structure of an experiment or investigation in terms of variables. Variables (whether they are independent, dependent or control) come in different guises. Identifying the type of variable in a scientific report, such as in the headlines above, helps to determine how the data should be analysed and how the question can be answered. So the type of variable matters.

The types of variables we need to consider here are:

- categoric
- ordered
- continuous.

3.1 Categoric variables

Any and every variable has associated with it certain 'values'. In our kettle example the variable 'the type of material' has values which are names such as plastic, steel or copper. Similarly 'the shape of the kettle' has values such as round or jug-shaped. These are the *values* of the variables 'the type of material' or 'the shape of the kettle'. They are values which cannot be measured by numbers; they can only be descriptive or categoric in that they relate to types of materials or

30

shapes. Variables of this kind are called CATEGORIC variables and will have values defined by words or labels. These sort of data are also referred to as NOMINAL data, that is to say they are 'named'. Nominal data are the weakest (or least powerful) level of measurement and, so, are normally only used when a better level of measurement, such as numerical measurement, is not possible or practical.

3.2 Ordered variables

Like categoric variables, ordered variables are essentially descriptive categories but the difference is that the categories can be ordered. Supposing the sizes of kettle elements are labelled small, standard, large and very large. These labels imply an *order* so that we know that standard is bigger than small and that large is bigger than standard. Compare these with the categoric variables, the type of the material (plastic, copper, steel). We cannot put the type of material in any logically meaningful order.

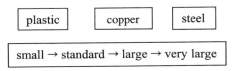

We can give ordered variables a number. For example, we could give the size of the kettle elements a number so that small = 1, standard = 2, large = 3 and very large = 4. But we need to be careful here because numbering categories can be misleading. Ranking the data like this can imply that 4 is twice as big as 2 whereas the size 4 element (very large) may not in fact be twice as big as the size 2 element (standard). So although we can put the size of the kettle elements in order, we cannot say *how much* bigger one size is than another. We shall see later that this has consequences for statistical analysis.

Ordered variables give ORDINAL data and are a 'stronger' (or more powerful) level of measurement than nominal data associated with categoric variables. It is important to note that even if ordered variables are numbered or ranked, the data should be treated as ordinal.

3.3 Continuous variables

In the kettle example, the variables 'time' and 'starting temperature' have numerical *values*: the time may be a value of 60 seconds or 15 minutes, while the starting temperature may be 10 °C. These variables are described as CONTINUOUS variables. That means that they can have absolutely any numerical value. The temperature can be 9 °C or 15 °C, or 22 °C, or 20.01 °C, or 20.000001 °C. Depending of course on how accurately we can measure, you can increase the number of decimal points for as long as you like. But there are no 'forbidden' values (except, of course, that water usually only exists as a liquid between 0 and 100 °C). Any *value* we assign to the variable is just one value of an infinite number. It follows that the interval between the values of continuous variables is meaningful and can be measured too, because each unit on the scale is equal. So if the boiling time for three kettles with the same quantity of water is 4, 8 and 10 minutes then we can do more than put them in order. We can say more than kettle 2 is better than kettle 1: we can say that it is twice as fast at boiling that quantity of water. We can also say that the difference between kettles 1 and 2 is twice as much as the difference between kettles 2 and 3. You may see this type of data referred to as INTERVAL data, because the interval or unit of measurement is meaningful and there are equal distances between the points on the scale. This makes these kind of data the strongest level of measurement.

Variable type	Variable values	Type of data	'Strength'/ 'power' of the level of measurement
categoric	names, labels	Nominal data	
ordered	ranked or ordered names or labels	Ordinal data	
continuous	any number, to any number of decimal places	Interval data	

☆ ☆ ☆ ☆ ☆ ☆

Before you read on, try to name the *type* of independent variable in the following three school science experiments:

1. How does current vary with different types of wire?
2. Investigate the relationship between the dissolving time of sugar and the size of the sugar particles.
3. Find out how respiration is related to exercise.

☆ ☆ ☆ ☆ ☆ ☆

In the first example, the type of wire such as copper, iron, etc. is a descriptive category, so this is a categoric variable. In the second, the size of the sugar particles in school science is often identified as coarse, fine, etc. and, so, is an ordered variable. Alternatively, if the type of sugar is identified by its common name and the order of grain size is unclear, such as might be the case with granulated and brown sugar, then it is a categoric variable. In the third example the type of the independent variable 'exercise' depends on how it is defined. It could be a categoric (running, cycling, gymnastics), a continuous (number of minutes of exercise) or an ordered (gentle, medium or hard exercise) variable.

☆ ☆ ☆ ☆ ☆ ☆

Now try the same thing with the following headline. You will need to define the independent variable:

Researchers link coffee to arthritis

☆ ☆ ☆ ☆ ☆ ☆

The independent variable is 'coffee'. It could be *ordered* by defining the number of cups of coffee taken per day. It could also be *continuous* if the intake of coffee was measured. The latter would be better and result in interval data which means that the relationship between coffee and arthritis can be defined more precisely.

3.4 Looking forward, looking back

Why does the variable type matter? It matters because it defines the level of measurement. The level of measurement determines how the results can be interpreted and used, as well as the reproducibility of the experiment. In general, the more quantitative (that is, measured by number) the better, because the power of the measurement is greater. In other words, a 'stronger' conclusion can be drawn from quantitative data. So if it is possible to measure a variable by making it a continuous variable, it is better to do so. Compare the following:

- Round plastic kettles take longer to boil 1 litre of cold tap water than plastic jug-type kettles.
- Round plastic kettles take 2.4 min longer to boil 1 litre of cold tap water than plastic jug-type kettles.

The second statement is more useful because we know the scale of the difference, namely, 2.4 minutes. The first statement only tells us that round kettles take longer to boil the water giving us no indication of *how much* longer: it could be 10 seconds or 10 minutes. The continuous data in the second statement allows us to decide whether a difference of 2.4 minutes matters depending on the reason for the test.

For example, if a company is marketing the plastic jug kettle, they might regard a fast boiling time as an important selling point.

In large areas of science, particularly in biological, medical and psychological experiments, numerical measurement may not be possible. In other instances, depending on the question or problem, measurement may not be necessary. Generally, however, scientific evidence is stronger if it is supported by continuous data. As we work through the book, you will be able to explore the full implications of the significance of measuring variables and compare it with handling evidence with categoric or ordered variables.

So, *looking forward*, when you construct the design of an experiment you should bear in mind that measurement is preferable wherever possible. *Looking back*, when you consider other people's evidence, you should ask yourself: did they measure the variables and if not, why not? If they did not measure, then what are the implications for handling the data?

You might want to add this point to your decision tree, something like this (do it in your own way):

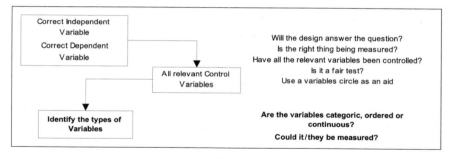

3.4.1 A note on other types of variables and data

There are other types of variables and data which you may come across in your practical work and which we will therefore describe briefly here.

'Derived' variables are those which have to be derived from others. An example is speed which is derived from distance (miles) and time (hours). It can be expressed as mph, or miles per hour.

The following table summarises all the types of variables we have discussed, the form that their values take and the types of data.

Variable type	Variable values	Type of data
Categoric	Names, labels	Nominal data
Ordered	Ranked or ordered names, labels	Ordinal data
Continuous	Any number, to any number of decimal places	Interval data
Other types of continuous data:		
Derived	Any number, to any number of decimal places	Interval data

3.5 Variables in investigations – the nine 'types'

3.5.1 Types of independent and dependent variables

As we saw in the last section, an investigation or experiment concerns the link between the independent and dependent variables. We also have just defined the three main types of variables: categoric, ordered and continuous. For any investigation or experiment, there are nine possible combinations of the three types of independent and dependent variables. These are shown in the following table and numbered 1–9:

	Dependent variable		
Independent variable	Categoric	Ordered	Continuous
Categoric	1	2	3
Ordered	4	5	6
Continuous	7	8	9

For clarity, to illustrate these nine different combinations, we shall use one investigation. The investigation is about the link between stomach powder and carbon dioxide. We shall also use a few other examples where appropriate. We shall begin with the three types of investigations with a categoric independent variable.

3.5.1.1 Investigation type 1: categoric–categoric (a categoric independent and a categoric dependent variable)

There are instances in science where measurement is not practical or possible. In a primary school, for instance, pupils might be testing different types of stomach powder in water to see whether or not carbon dioxide is emitted and, given limited resources, it may not be possible (or necessary, depending on the purpose of the lesson) to measure the amount of carbon dioxide.

	may/may not affect	
TYPE OF STOMACH POWDER **e.g. type A, type B, etc.**	⟶	**CARBON DIOXIDE** **yes, no**
(categoric independent variable)		(categoric dependent variable)

The resulting table of data might look something like this:

Type of stomach powder	Carbon dioxide
Type A	Yes
Type B	Yes
Type C	No
Type D	Yes

The conclusions from such data are limited. Here, the most we can say is that particular types of stomach powder (Types A, B and D) give off carbon dioxide and that Type C does not.

Here is another example, testing substances for acidity or alkalinity:

Chemical	Acid/Alkali/Neither
Water	Neither
Vinegar	Acid
Antacid pill	Alkali

Although we now have three categories, the conclusion can still only be descriptive: a categorisation of chemicals into acids, alkalis or neither. In some circumstances, depending on the purpose of the exercise, this level of measurement may be sufficient.

3.5.1.2 Investigation type 2: categoric–ordered

In this type of investigation, the level of measurement of the dependent variable is greater in that it can be ordered. In the stomach powder example, descriptive categories can be used which allow the powders to be ordered according to the amount of carbon dioxide emitted.

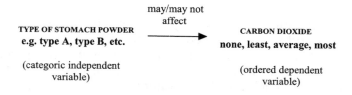

The data will now look like this:

Type of stomach powder	Carbon dioxide
Type C	None
Type B	Least
Type D	Average
Type A	Most

Although the stomach powders can be ordered as in the table, the descriptive categories are rather vague and subjective so that the conclusions are limited. Another example is of a medical test of different types of anti-depressant drugs, where one possible measure of the effect of the drug is to ask the patient if s/he feels: awful, not too bad, happy and so on. Quantitative data are not possible but the effect of the drug on the patient's mood can be ordered from bad to good:

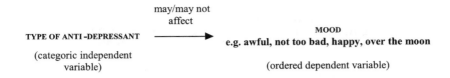

Again, it is clear that, although the categories of mood can be ordered, they may not be objective or mutually exclusive (i.e. they may overlap) which limits the strength of the conclusion.

3.5.1.3 Investigation type 3: categoric–continuous
In this type of investigation, in the stomach powder example, the quantity of carbon dioxide emitted becomes continuous because it is measured in cm^3.

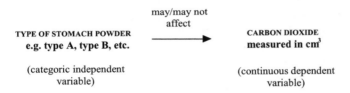

The data now has numerical values for the dependent variable:

Type of stomach powder	Carbon dioxide (cm^3)
Type C	0
Type B	12
Type D	28
Type A	56

We can make a much more definite statement in that we can see *exactly* how much carbon dioxide is emitted. Notice that in this table, there is one column of *names* and one of *numbers* because we have a categoric and a continuous variable.

We can then consider the three types of investigations with an ordered independent variable.

3.5.1.4 Investigation type 4: ordered–categoric
In this type of investigation, a little more information is available about the independent variable so that the values can be ordered. In the stomach powder example, the different types of powder can be ordered by the amount of carbonate each contains. But as in type 1, the dependent variable is categoric so that the conclusions are limited.

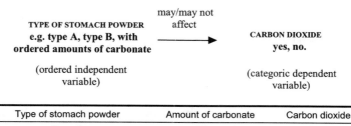

Type of stomach powder	Amount of carbonate	Carbon dioxide
Type C	None	No
Type B	Least	Yes
Type D	Average	Yes
Type A	Most	Yes

The relationship between the amount of carbonate and carbon dioxide may seem obvious but it serves to illustrate the design. Another perhaps more meaningful example is the medical one we used before. In terms of this design, we could explore the relationship between the amount of a chemical in different types of anti-depressant drug which may or may not be related to whether or not the patient's depression improves:

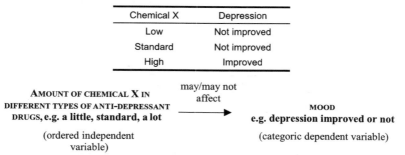

Again, the level of measurement of the dependent variable is weak and the conclusions are limited. The results enable us to say that a high level of chemical X appears to improve depression but that standard and low levels do not.

3.5.1.5 Investigation type 5: ordered–ordered
In some circumstances, both the independent and the dependent variable can be ordered:

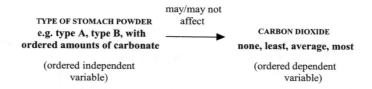

Type of stomach powder	Amount of carbonate	Carbon dioxide
Type C	None	None
Type B	Least	Least
Type D	Average	Average
Type A	Most	Most

Again, because the relationship seems rather obvious, we shall look more closely at the medical example:

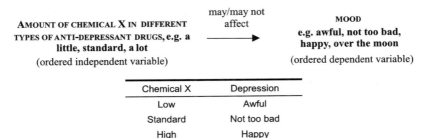

Chemical X	Depression
Low	Awful
Standard	Not too bad
High	Happy

Here, the results could enable us to say how the three different amounts of chemical X affect depression in terms of the mood categories and so we know more than we did in the last example (type 4). There is more of an indication that the anti-depressant drug may be effective.

3.5.1.6 Investigation type 6: ordered–continuous

As in type 3, continuous data obtained from measuring the dependent variable allows us to see *exactly* how much carbon dioxide is emitted by each type of stomach powder and, because the independent variable is ordered, we can look for a pattern between the amount of carbonate and the volume of carbon dioxide. The results show that the more carbonate the stomach powder contains, the more carbon dioxide is emitted.

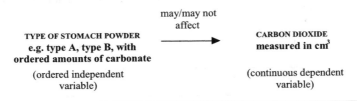

Type of stomach powder	Amount of carbonate	Carbon dioxide (cm^3)
Type C	None	0
Type B	Least	12
Type D	Average	28
Type A	Most	56

The last three types of investigations are those associated with a continuous independent variable.

3.5.1.7 Investigation type 7: continuous–categoric

The independent variable can be continuous if, for example, the percentage of carbonate in each type of stomach powder can be measured. The dependent variable in this design is categoric limiting the conclusions. All we can say is that if there is no carbonate, as in stomach powder type C, then no carbon dioxide is emitted and if there is 10 per cent or more carbonate then carbon dioxide is emitted. (Note that we cannot say whether a stomach powder with 5 per cent carbonate would emit carbon dioxide or not).

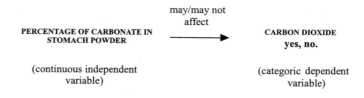

Type of stomach powder	Percentage of carbonate	Carbon dioxide (cm^3)
Type C	0	No
Type B	10	Yes
Type D	25	Yes
Type A	50	Yes

In the medical example, the relationship between the strength of an anti-depressant drug and whether or not it improves depression can be explored:

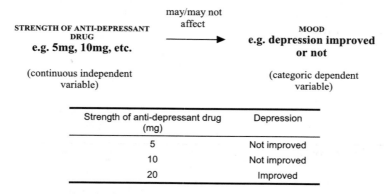

Strength of anti-depressant drug (mg)	Depression
5	Not improved
10	Not improved
20	Improved

We can say that this particular anti-depressant if used at a strength of 10 mg or less is unlikely to improve depression.

3.5.1.8 Investigation type 8: continuous–ordered

When the dependent variable can be ordered, the conclusions are stronger. Here we can detect a pattern in that the greater the percentage of carbonate, the greater the amount of carbon dioxide emitted in terms of the four ordered categories (none, least, average, most). We can also say that a stomach powder with 50 per cent carbonate appears to give off the most carbon dioxide (compared to the other three types).

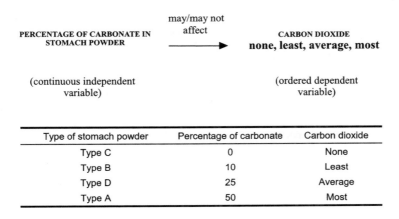

		may/may not affect		
PERCENTAGE OF CARBONATE IN STOMACH POWDER	→		CARBON DIOXIDE none, least, average, most
(continuous independent variable)			(ordered dependent variable)

Type of stomach powder	Percentage of carbonate	Carbon dioxide
Type C	0	None
Type B	10	Least
Type D	25	Average
Type A	50	Most

The medical example would look like this:

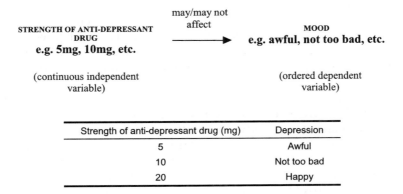

		may/may not affect		
STRENGTH OF ANTI-DEPRESSANT DRUG e.g. 5mg, 10mg, etc.	→		MOOD e.g. awful, not too bad, etc.
(continuous independent variable)			(ordered dependent variable)

Strength of anti-depressant drug (mg)	Depression
5	Awful
10	Not too bad
20	Happy

The results here would enable us to say how the strength of the anti-depressant drug affects mood. Given a big enough sample (an issue which we will address in Chapter 8), we could determine, for example, the minimum dose that would make most patients 'happy'. In a situation like this, where the state of depression cannot be directly measured, the strongest data possible for the dependent variable is at the ordinal level of measurement.

3.5.1.9 Investigation type 9: continuous–continuous

Where both variables can be measured quantitatively, then the relationship between the two variables can be explored fully. This is the ideal experiment but, as already noted, not always possible and indeed not always necessary. If we consider the stomach powder example, then because we have numbers in both columns, we can look for a mathematical pattern or relationship. From this we can predict or model what would happen with theoretical stomach powders without actually testing them.

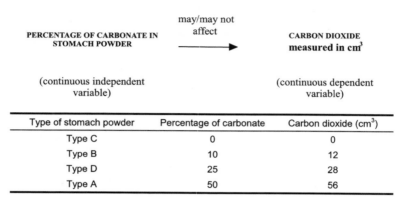

Type of stomach powder	Percentage of carbonate	Carbon dioxide (cm^3)
Type C	0	0
Type B	10	12
Type D	25	28
Type A	50	56

From the table, we can see that when the percentage of carbonate doubles (from 25 per cent to 50 per cent), so does the amount of carbon dioxide emitted (28cm^3 to 56cm^3). If we were to check out this relationship (for example, by using more types of powder), we might then be able to predict the amount of carbon dioxide given off by any stomach powder if we knew its percentage composition of carbonate.

An investigation with a continuous independent and a continuous dependent variable is the strongest combination of variables in that it allows the relationship between the two variables to be explored in detail. Patterns can be looked for and if found, may be expressed mathematically. From these patterns, predictions can be made. We shall be looking closely at this sort of relationship and more complicated relationships in later sections.

3.5.2 Types of control variables

Just as it is better to make independent and dependent variables continuous wherever possible, the same applies to control variables. Returning to the kettle example, compare these two statements:

- Round plastic kettles take 2.4 min longer to boil 1 litre of cold tap water than plastic jug-type kettles.
- Round plastic kettles take 2.4 min longer to boil 1 litre of tap water *at 10 °C* than plastic jug-type kettles.

In the first statement, the 'cold' water in different laboratories could vary by several degrees. Different boiling times could result from this variation. In the second statement, the temperature is specified which means that the test can be replicated using exactly the same temperature of water. So, defining the control variable as continuous means that the reproducibility and hence the reliability of the data is better.

☆ ☆ ☆ ☆ ☆ ☆

Try thinking about how some of the control variables could be continuous in the three school investigations:

1. How does current vary with different types of wire?
2. Investigate the relationship between the dissolving time of sugar and the size of the sugar particles.
3. Find out how respiration is related to exercise.

Take the fluoride headline again:

Government backs fluoride
for all

The independent variable might be water to which fluoride has been added compared to water without added fluoride. The dependent variable could be a measure of tooth decay in the population. Think about the control variables and how they could be made continuous. A variables circle can help to clarify your thoughts – add some control variables to your own variables circle.

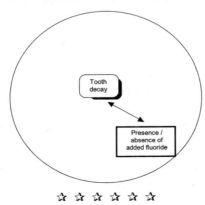

Tooth decay

Presence / absence of added fluoride

☆ ☆ ☆ ☆ ☆ ☆

There are many possible control variables. Two examples of continuous control variables are the time period that the population has had fluoride added to their drinking water or the quantity of fluoride added to the water.

3.6 Summary

- In this section, we have considered three types of variables, namely, categoric, ordered and continuous variables which result in nominal, ordinal and interval data respectively. Interval data is the strongest or most powerful level of measurement.
- There are nine possible combinations of these three types of variables. Depending on the question, it is usually preferable whenever possible to design an experiment with continuous variables to produce interval data. This applies particularly to the dependent variable but also to the independent and the control variables:

	Dependent variable		
Independent variable	Categoric	Ordered	Continuous
Categoric	1	2	3
Ordered	4	5	6
Continuous	7	8	9

- An investigation of type 9 where both the independent and dependent variables are continuous provides stronger data or more useful information than any of the other types of designs. But please note that in some instances, the purpose of the experiment may mean that such a design is unnecessary and indeed, measurement at this level is not always possible.

To make sure you understand the ideas presented in this chapter, see if you can locate the following investigations in the grid above:

1. How does current vary with different types of wire (i.e. different materials)?
2. Investigate the relationship between the dissolving time of sugar and the size of the sugar particles (defined as very fine, fine, medium, coarse and very coarse).

3. Find out how respiration (breathing rate) is related to exercise (time spent on cardiovascular exercise).

Now try locating these two headlines in the same way:

Vanilla dulls sweet craving

After nicotine patches for people who want to quit smoking come vanilla patches for chocolate addicts who want to lose weight.

A study at St George's hospital in Tooting, south London, has found that vanilla-scented patches can significantly reduce the appetite for chocolate, sweet foods and drinks.

Poor air quality puts steelworks in bad odour with locals
New research intensifies fears over effects of pollution

You will probably find this more difficult. First you will need to define the independent and dependent variables. In the first article the variables could be defined as:

- *Independent variable*: chocolate addicts wearing vanilla-scented patches and chocolate addicts who are not wearing vanilla-scented patches.
- *Dependent variable*: quantity of sweet items (e.g. weight) ingested over a given period of time.

Now identify what *type* of variable each of these is and then locate the investigation in the grid.

Try the second example about pollution yourself.

☆ ☆ ☆ ☆ ☆ ☆

Where are you?

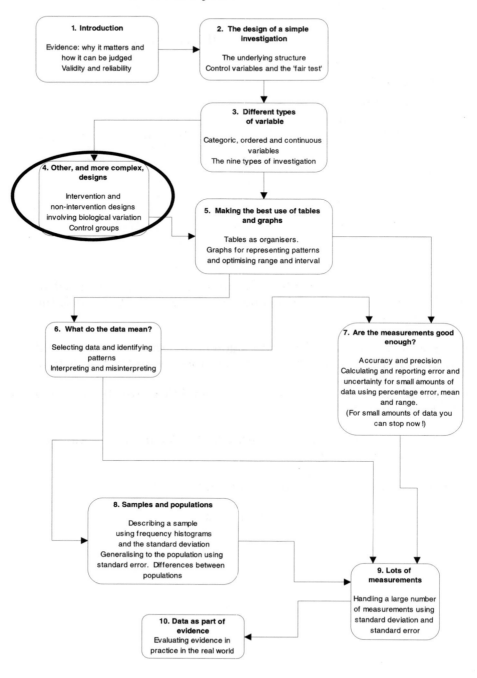

1. Introduction

Evidence: why it matters and how it can be judged
Validity and reliability

2. The design of a simple investigation

The underlying structure
Control variables and the 'fair test'

3. Different types of variable

Categoric, ordered and continuous variables
The nine types of investigation

4. Other, and more complex, designs

Intervention and non-intervention designs involving biological variation
Control groups

5. Making the best use of tables and graphs

Tables as organisers.
Graphs for representing patterns and optimising range and interval

6. What do the data mean?

Selecting data and identifying patterns
Interpreting and misinterpreting

7. Are the measurements good enough?

Accuracy and precision
Calculating and reporting error and uncertainty for small amounts of data using percentage error, mean and range.
(For small amounts of data you can stop now !)

8. Samples and populations

Describing a sample using frequency histograms and the standard deviation
Generalising to the population using standard error. Differences between populations

9. Lots of measurements

Handling a large number of measurements using standard deviation and standard error

10. Data as part of evidence
Evaluating evidence in practice in the real world

Chapter 4

Other, and more complex, designs

Introduction

Field studies?	Randomised control trials (RCTs)?

In Chapter 2, we looked closely at the simplest and 'cleanest' type of experimental design. In this simple type of design we saw that, by keeping all the relevant control variables the same, the relationship between the independent and dependent variable can be isolated. This is often not possible. This kind of investigation or experiment is usually done in the laboratory, mainly because it is easier to control variables in a contained environment. In this chapter, we shall look at other kinds of design, including field studies and randomised control trials, some of which are done in the laboratory and some outside.

4.1 Other types of 'intervention' investigations

In the simplest type of investigation in Chapter 2, the investigator *actively* changes the independent variable to explore its effect on the dependent variable. Any experiment in which an investigator changes something or intervenes in some way can be thought of as an 'intervention' investigation. Consider these examples:

1. How does the rate of a chemical reaction depend on temperature?
2. Find out how much water tomato seedlings need for optimal growth.
3. How do elephants affect vegetation in a National Park?
4. 'New drug will boost breast cancer fight.'

These are all intervention investigations because something is *actively* or *intentionally* changed or added or taken away. We shall look at each of these investigations in turn since they illustrate a range of types of designs of investigation.

1 How does the rate of a chemical reaction depend on temperature?

Identify the independent and dependent variable. Think of some of the control variables (you may find sketching a variables circle helpful).

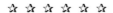

You will probably recognise that this is another example of the simplest type of design, where the relevant variables such as the mass of the chemical, the volume of the acid, the stirring, etc. can be reasonably easily controlled. It is a typical school science experiment usually carried out in the laboratory. The investigator actively intervenes by changing the temperature. The independent variable is temperature and the dependent variable is the the rate at which the reaction proceeds.

☆ ☆ ☆ ☆ ☆ ☆

2 How much water do tomato plants need for growth?

This investigation could be carried out in a laboratory/heated greenhouse. Let us suppose that we begin the experiment with 20 healthy seedlings, 10 cm tall, raised in pots in the same way. Each of the following amounts of water are applied daily to five seedlings:

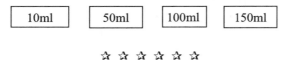

| 10ml | 50ml | 100ml | 150ml |

☆ ☆ ☆ ☆ ☆ ☆

Decide why this is an intervention investigation, identify the independent and dependent variable and think about the control variables.

☆ ☆ ☆ ☆ ☆ ☆

In this investigation, the intervention is the change in the independent variable, the daily application of water. The dependent variable is some measure of plant growth, such as the height of the plant or the number, or the colour, of the leaves. The control variables include the species of tomato plant, the size of the pot, the type and quantity of compost and the time of watering. All these variables can be kept the same.

But what about light? The plants are exposed to normal light conditions, i.e. kept in daylight during the day and in darkness at night. Notice here that the control variable, light, is not kept *the same* – the degree of light is *not* held constant. But all the plants are subjected to the same light regime. It would, of course, be possible to keep the degree of light the same by using artificial light. But let us suppose that this is a trial for ordinary gardeners with outdoor greenhouses with no artificial light. Then it is sensible to carry out the trial with conditions as close to reality as possible so that the results will be applicable to normal conditions.

Another feature of this investigation is that for each value of the independent variable (amount of water), five seedlings were used. It would not be sensible to use just one seedling for each watering regime because we would expect there to be some biological variation between the seedlings even though they were raised in similar conditions. So a group of five seedlings was used. The investigator decided that a sample of five seedlings would be *representative* of the tomato seedling population.

To recap, in this investigation, light is an example of a different type of control variable from the type of control variable described in chapter 2. This type of control variable is *not* kept the same but allowed to vary but *it varies in the same way for each change in the independent variable*.

This investigation also illustrates the use of a group as a unit of the independent variable. Using a group as opposed to a single individual/unit is often appropriate when variation between measurements is significant. This not only applies to plants and animals in biology but is also the case in many other areas of science. In chemistry, for example, in sampling a large quantity of an unknown chemical, it would be sensible to test more than one sample, or in geology to sample more than one piece of rock. In any kind of manufacturing business, quality control involves sampling the product to check its performance. Supposing a company manufactures chocolate bars or tennis balls. The quality control department will run experiments checking the performance or quality of a sample of chocolate bars or tennis balls. This is the same principle as the sample of seedling tomatoes. We will consider the issue of choosing a big enough sample later, in Chapter 8.

3 How do elephants affect the vegetation in a National Park?
Unlike the two previous examples, this is not a laboratory study! It is a study which can really only be carried out sensibly in natural conditions, i.e. the elephants' normal environment. Investigations carried

out in natural conditions are called 'field studies'. (Note that does not mean that the experiment has to be done in a field. For instance, a field study of office workers would take place in the office.)

One way of studying the effect of elephants on their habitat, which has been done, is to exclude them from measured areas of vegetation by digging large ditches around the area. (The ditches prevent elephants entering the area while allowing most other grazing and browsing animals, who can jump across the ditches, access to the vegetation.) These areas are called 'exclosures'. The vegetation in these areas is measured at the beginning of the investigation and at regular intervals during the study and compared with marked areas of the same size with similar vegetation where elephants have free access.

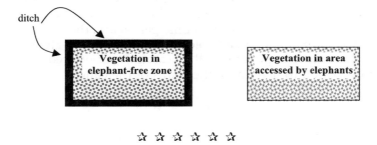

☆ ☆ ☆ ☆ ☆ ☆

Consider the structure of this experiment. What is the intervention? Draw a variable circle and mark the independent variable (IV), the dependent variable (DV) and some control variables (CV). Decide whether the control variables can be kept the same or if they should be allowed to vary.

☆ ☆ ☆ ☆ ☆ ☆

The intervention is the exclusion of elephants from the areas of vegetation or exclosures. Notice that the intervention here is taking something away (elephants). The independent variable then is the presence or absence of elephants. The dependent variable could be the change in number, type or condition of species of plants.

What about the control variables? Some, like the timing of the measurement of the vegetation, can and should be kept the same. But one of the main control variables is the weather which includes variables such as rainfall, temperature, humidity and wind. These variables, like the light in the last example, cannot be held constant. But if the two areas of vegetation are located close together, then the weather conditions will vary in the same way. This type of control variable is very common in field studies where it is neither feasible nor sensible to keep some of the control variables the same.

Similarly we could run the tomato trial as a field study by growing tomato seedlings outside in four marked areas of land in close proximity. The watering regime would be the same as before. All the control variables to do with the weather would change in an unpredictable way but *change in the same way* for all the seedlings.

4 New drug will boost breast cancer fight

> New drug will boost breast cancer fight

We can envisage that the design behind this headline might consist of two groups of patients diagnosed with breast cancer. One group will be given the new drug for a specified time period and the other group will be treated with the standard 'older' drugs normally given to breast cancer patients. The patients will be carefully monitored over a specified time period to determine the status of the cancer.

☆ ☆ ☆ ☆ ☆ ☆

Identify the intervention and the key variables.

☆ ☆ ☆ ☆ ☆ ☆

The intervention is the administration of the new drug so that the independent variable is the type of drug – new or old taken by breast cancer patients. The dependent variable is the status of their cancer. Some of the control variables could be the sex and age of the patients, their other medical conditions, the other drugs they are taking, their smoking status, the type of diet they follow, their fitness level and the stage of the cancer at diagnosis. It is possible to decide on a fixed value for each of these variables and then aim to keep them the same. So, for example, only 40-year-old very fit non-smoking vegetarian women diagnosed with the early onset of cancer with no other medical condition and taking no other drugs would be included in the experiment. Although the experiment can be done with this kind of simple design, it is clear that a lot of patients would be excluded. To make matters more complicated, there are a lot more relevant control variables which cause individuals to vary such as blood type, blood pressure and genetic make-up so that it would be very difficult to strictly control *all* these variables.

The design behind a headline like this is more likely to be a 'Randomised Control Trial' (RCT) which is regarded as the 'gold standard' in medicine. But note that the RCT is also used in other areas such as psychology or zoology or botany, in fact in any area where there is variation in a large number of the relevant control variables.

In a randomised control trial, the investigator might first decide to control one or two relevant variables in the usual way for particular reasons. For example, the trial might exclude those patients who have already been treated with cancer drugs and restrict both groups to newly diagnosed breast cancer patients. Previous cancer treatment might influence how patients react to the new drug, so its effect would not be clear. Once these controls or conditions are selected, then those patients who meet those conditions are randomly allocated to either:

- the 'experimental' group, which in this example is those patients who are treated with the new drug, or
- the 'control' group which is the group of patients receiving the usual or standard treatment.

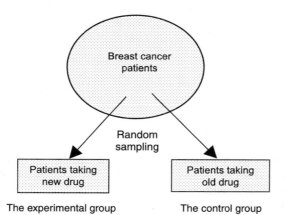

An example of the design of a Randomised Control Trial or RCT

By using random sampling and a big enough sample, it is assumed that the two groups will be roughly equivalent or matched on the relevant control variables. Random sampling and the size of the sample are both ideas which are very important in understanding scientific evidence. But we will defer the whole issue of sampling for now and return to it later in Chapter 8.

In the example above, notice the use of the word control in 'control group'. It bears little relationship to the meaning of control in control variables. Instead, it refers to the group who represent the *normal* or *untreated* condition.

This is an example of a field study which is also a randomised control trial. A randomised control trial is a design which divides the values of the independent variable into experimental and control groups. It is commonly used when there are a large number of control variables which could be relevant. There can be more than one experimental group in a RCT. In the example above there could be one experimental group taking a low dose of the new drug and a second experimental group taking a higher dose of the new drug.

We should also note here that *control groups* are not restricted to randomised control trials. In any investigation where a group in the natural or usual condition is used for comparison with a group (or groups) exposed to an intervention, then the untreated group is called 'the control group'.

☆ ☆ ☆ ☆ ☆ ☆

To make sure you understand these ideas, in each of the following, identify the intervention, the key variables, the nature of the control variables (are they kept the same or allowed to vary?) and whether or not there is a control group.

1. A tomato trial outside in which 10 tomato seedlings are exposed to the following watering regimes:

| No water | 10ml | 50ml | 100ml | 150ml |

2. The badger culling trial.

There is some evidence that badgers are a source of infection of TB in cattle. A trial was set up in the south of England using 10 sites where the incidence of TB in cattle had been relatively high. In each site three areas were given a different treatment. The three treatments were:

- Treatment 1: as many badgers as possible were trapped and killed.
- Treatment 2: only badger 'families' associated with farms which had cattle with TB were trapped and killed.
- Treatment 3: no badgers were killed but they were surveyed to record badger activity.

3. Now apply the same ideas to this advertisement.

Slimtone is an Abdominal Training System. It's not like any other muscle toning system you've ever used before. Slimtone technology is clinically proven to work by exercising all the stomach muscles. It's the new smart way to a firmer, flatter stomach.

☆ ☆ ☆ ☆ ☆ ☆

4.2 Non-intervention investigations

So far, although we have considered a wide range of investigations, they have all had one thing in common: there was an *active intervention* of some kind. There are other types of experiments particularly (but not only) in biology where the aim is to explore relationships or look for a difference or change in the natural environment, where an intervention would be inappropriate.

In this type of 'non-intervention' investigation, the investigator decides to gather data on variables of particular interest and sometimes also on those that *might* be relevant. The data are often used retrospectively to answer a question. The investigator does not make any changes to the natural situation: there is no intervention. These investigations or experiments are often, but not always, field studies. Here are some examples:

1. How does the vitamin C content of a type of apple change between the time of picking and the sell by date?
2. Are two samples of wood mice different from each other in terms of body weight?
3. Is there a significant difference between the treatment of cancer in area X compared to area Y?
4. What factors affect the behaviour of a species of gazelle in a national park?

The first investigation is looking for change over time while investigations 2 and 3 are looking for significant difference. By way of example of the structure of non-intervention investigations, we shall look at the fourth investigation. It is a typical field study.

4.2.1 What factors affect the behaviour of a species of gazelle in a particular national park?

In very open investigations like this, the investigator will have several possible factors or variables in mind from studies of other similar animals. The investigator then goes out and collects data on all these variables. They might include the variables shown in the circle at the top of the next page.

The situation here is very complex. We can't 'experiment' with the animals by creating different habitats for practical reasons, to say nothing of ethical/animal rights issues. So we only have one option: to collect data 'in the field', with as little disturbance as possible to the ecosystem that is being observed. By its very nature, such an exercise is very expensive. It requires that somebody (or a team of people) spends

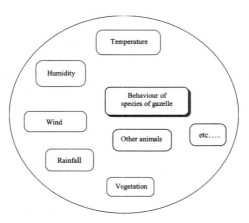

many hours observing or videoing gazelle behaviour as well as measuring a whole host of other variables. Many of these measurements have to be taken at frequent intervals. The temperature, for example, will vary through the day or the gazelles may wander into different vegetation zones. It is normal in such circumstances to collect as much data as possible on as many potentially significant variables as possible, just in case they are important. The end result is a mass of data on perhaps 10 or 20 variables over a considerable period of time.

What follows is a subset of measurements and observations resulting from the first 15 minutes of a day's observation of a group of Grant's gazelle in Kenya. The data are coded for ease of recording.

Date:....................

Time	Temperature °C*	Relative humidity (%) *	Male	Female	Young	Behaviour							Vegetation type	Rain	Cloud cover	Other animals within sight
						S	SF	W	WF	L	F					
7.00	18	92	1	8	3	1	2	6	2	1		4	2	3	5
7.05	18	92	1	8	3	4	3	4		1		5	2	3	5,6
7.10	18	92	1	8	3		7	2	1		2	5	2	2	2,6
7.15	18	92	1	8	3	2		2	8			5	2	2	2
etc..															

*Recorded at 30 min intervals

KEY:
Activity: S = standing, SF = standing feeding, W = walking, WF = walking feeding, L = lying, F = fighting, etc.
Vegetation type: 4 = open grassland, 5 = grass and shrubs, etc.
Rain: 1 = rain, 2 = dry
Cloud cover: 0-25% = 1, 25-50% = 2, 50-75% = 3, etc.
Other animals: 2 = warthog, 5 = wildebeest, 6 = impala, etc.

The two main types of groups in which Grant's gazelles live were observed every month for 12 months so that the final data consist of twenty-four days of observations of group behaviour at five minute intervals.

How can we structure an investigation from data of this kind? First, we need to break down the question: 'What factors affect the behaviour of a species of gazelle in a particular national park?' We need to define this open question into one or more specific questions that select particular factors which, from our observation, we might suspect are affecting gazelle behaviour. For example:

- Does *temperature*
- Does *humidity*
- Does the *type of vegetation*   affect the behaviour of this
- Does the *presence of other animals*   species of gazelle?
- etc.

Each of these questions identifies a different independent variable.

Let us look more closely at the first question choosing temperature as the independent variable. You may have got the impression from your observation that gazelles are more active in the cool than in the heat – sensible behaviour! So we are aiming to investigate this question:

> **What is the effect of temperature on behaviour?**

The next step is to isolate the data on temperature and behaviour, ignoring the rest of the data for now. There are a variety of ways to proceed. For instance, we might simplify the data by combining some of the categories. We could divide the behaviour categories into those in which the gazelles are moving around or 'active' (anything to do with walking or running) and those in which they are stationary or 'static' (anything to do with lying or standing). We will ignore the remaining categories such as fighting etc. for now. We can simplify temperature by focusing on the periods of the day when the temperature is hotter, i.e. in the middle of the day, and when it is cooler, i.e. early morning and late afternoon. We can choose a specific temperature as a boundary to define this – here we have chosen 22 °C. So hours when the average temperature is equal to or greater than 22 °C are 'hotter' and those which are less than 22 °C are 'cooler'.

	Hotter hours (≥22°C)	Cooler hours (<22°C)
Active	55	80
Static	45	20

Figures represent mean percentage activity of gazelles/hour

The table shows that our hunch that gazelles are more active at cooler times of day appears to be correct.

But look back at the variables circle.

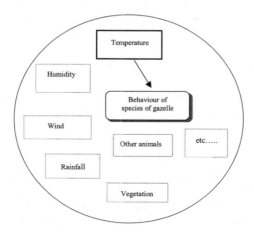

It could be that some of the other factors we thought might influence behaviour could be equally, or more, important than temperature in affecting gazelle behaviour. So far we have not controlled any of these factors. Suppose we decide to control rainfall. We can do this by examining gazelle behaviour at hotter and cooler times of day *only when it was not raining.*

We might then decide to refine our question still further and control the type of vegetation by looking at the effect of temperature when there was no rain and *in only one type of vegetation.* So now we are controlling two variables: rainfall and vegetation type. The problem is of course you are excluding more and more of the data as you narrow the question and increase the number of controls. You might like to think of it as a sort of 'filtering' exercise. Eventually you will reach a point at which there is not enough data to give meaningful results.

Looking again at the circle of variables you will see that any of the factors (apart from the dependent variable, behaviour) could be an independent variable or a control variable. For instance, if instead of temperature we had chosen to investigate the effect of the type of vegetation on gazelle behaviour, we would then make the vegetation type the independent variable. We might then control the temperature (e.g. to within 10°C bands) or rainfall.

In this kind of non-intervention study the nature of the data means that the types of the variables can be interchanged. We are in effect creating questions which we can investigate from the data. If we find a relationship which is of interest, we might then do a more focused field study to test out the relationship more fully.

☆ ☆ ☆ ☆ ☆ ☆

Draw variables circles for the three other non-intervention investigations on page 55.

☆ ☆ ☆ ☆ ☆ ☆

4.3 Summary

In this chapter, the focus has been on experiments or investigations which have a more complex structure and design. These include:

- intervention investigations in which some of the control variables are allowed to change but *change in the same way* for each value of the independent variable;
- randomised control trials in which, by using large enough samples and randomisation, it is assumed that the control variables will be matched between the experimental and 'control' groups;
- investigations in which there is no active intervention but in which the 'natural' environment provides the data. The investigator decides which data to collect;
- some non-intervention investigations, and particularly field studies, result in a large quantity of data which allow for exploration of several independent variables. The independent and control variables can be interchangeable such that the data may be used to create questions retrospectively. Data are selected to answer specific questions and control variables are applied in a 'filtering' manner.

4.4 Looking forward, looking back

In more complex investigations and experiments, in looking forward or looking back, it is even more essential to make sure that data are, or will be available for the relevant variables so that the investigation will be valid and the question answerable.

We cannot add much to our decision tree but note that we now have a much broader definition of control variables.

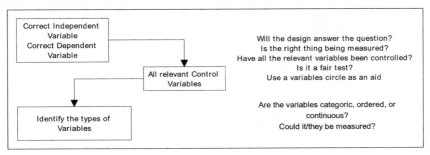

Where are you?

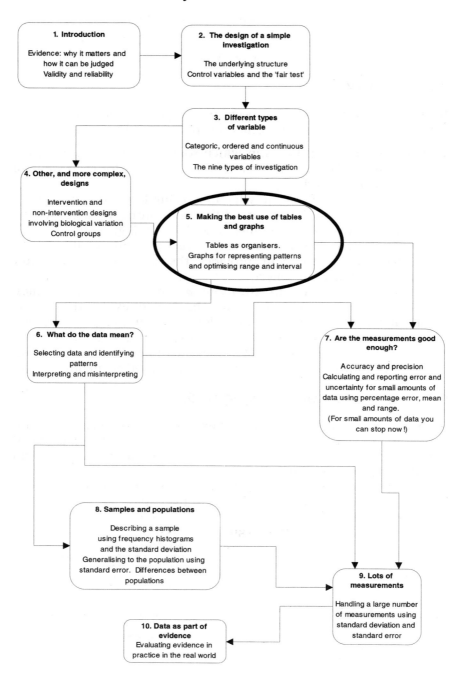

1. Introduction

Evidence: why it matters and how it can be judged
Validity and reliability

2. The design of a simple investigation

The underlying structure
Control variables and the 'fair test'

3. Different types of variable

Categoric, ordered and continuous variables
The nine types of investigation

4. Other, and more complex, designs

Intervention and non-intervention designs involving biological variation
Control groups

5. Making the best use of tables and graphs

Tables as organisers.
Graphs for representing patterns and optimising range and interval

6. What do the data mean?

Selecting data and identifying patterns
Interpreting and misinterpreting

7. Are the measurements good enough?

Accuracy and precision
Calculating and reporting error and uncertainty for small amounts of data using percentage error, mean and range.
(For small amounts of data you can stop now !)

8. Samples and populations

Describing a sample using frequency histograms and the standard deviation
Generalising to the population using standard error. Differences between populations

9. Lots of measurements

Handling a large number of measurements using standard deviation and standard error

10. Data as part of evidence
Evaluating evidence in practice in the real world

Chapter 5

Making the best use
of tables and graphs

Introduction

In the last three chapters we considered a number of possible designs of investigations or experiments in terms of their variable structure and the function of control groups. In this chapter, we take a look at tables and graphs. Tables and graphs are typically seen as adornments at worst, or display tools at best. They are used as ways of tidying up and recording data that has been jotted down haphazardly or as an afterthought after the practical part of an experiment has been done. Below we shall see that tables and graphs can, and should, be seen as more proactive than this.

5.1 Tables

Tables have a dual purpose. They can be used as:

- an *organiser* for the investigation;
- a way of *presenting data in a report*.

As an organiser, a table can be used as an essential element of the experimental plan. It is best to construct a table *before you begin* practical work and use it as an *organiser* for the experiment. The structure of a table is linked to the variable structure as shown in the circle and table at the top of page 63.

(We will construct tables with the variables in this order [the independent in the first column and the dependent variables in the remaining columns] throughout this book; but it is no more than a convention and other ways of organising data will be encountered in the press and elsewhere.)

We shall explore this link more fully in the section that follows.

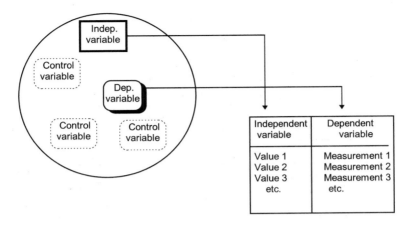

Tables are also, of course, a way of reporting the actual data *after* an investigation. If necessary a table may have to be redrawn, for example, summarising the data and/or using a computer. The table *rarely tells you anything about the control variables*; this is an important omission and one to which we shall return later.

5.2 Table design

In Chapter 3, we explored the design of investigations with nine different combinations of types of independent and dependent variable (see next table). These combinations of types of variables in an experiment determine the most appropriate choice of table and graph.

	Dependent variable		
Independent variable	Categoric	Ordered	Continuous
Categoric	1	2	3
Ordered	4	5	6
Continuous	7	8	9

The nine combinations of independent and dependent variables

Below, we have reproduced the tables used in Chapter 3 as examples for each type of investigation. By looking at all these tables at once, the combination of categoric, ordered and continuous independent and dependent variables is reflected in the format of the table. So, for example, whenever there is a continuous independent variable, there will be numbers in the left-hand column of the table. Or, whenever there is an ordered dependent variable, there will be an ordered list of some kind in the right-hand column.

				DEPENDENT				
		Categoric			Ordered			Continuous
INDEPENDENT								

Type 1

Type of stomach powder	Carbon dioxide
Type A	Yes
Type B	Yes
Type C	No
Type D	Yes

Type 2

Type of stomach powder	Carbon dioxide
Type C	None
Type B	Least
Type D	Average
Type A	Most

Type 3

Type of stomach powder	Carbon dioxide (cm^3)
Type C	0
Type B	12
Type D	28
Type A	56

Type 4

Amount of carbonate	Carbon dioxide
None (C)	No
Least (B)	Yes
Average (D)	Yes
Most (A)	Yes

Type 5

Amount of carbonate	Carbon dioxide
None (C)	None
Least (B)	Least
Average (D)	Average
Most (A)	Most

Type 6

Amount of carbonate	Carbon dioxide (cm^3)
None (C)	0
Least (B)	12
Average (D)	28
Most (A)	56

Type 7

Percentage of carbonate	Carbon dioxide
0 (C)	No
10 (B)	Yes
25 (D)	Yes
50 (A)	Yes

Type 8

Percentage of carbonate	Carbon dioxide
0 (C)	None
10 (B)	Least
25 (D)	Average
50 (A)	Most

Type 9

Percentage of carbonate	Carbon dioxide (cm^3)
0 (C)	0
10 (B)	12
25 (D)	28
50 (A)	56

(Independent column labels: Categoric — Types 1, 2, 3; Ordered — Types 4, 5, 6; Continuous — Types 7, 8, 9.)

For any of these investigations, a table can be constructed as soon as the question is defined with the independent variable in the left-hand column and the right-hand column labelled with a heading ready to receive the measurements.

5.2.1 Using and presenting a table with a categoric independent variable (types 1, 2 and 3)

Suppose the question is:

> Which type of stomach powder will produce the greatest volume of carbon dioxide?

The independent variable is categoric, with values that are the names of each type of stomach powder. Suppose we have no way of measuring carbon dioxide quantitatively but, instead, we can estimate the relative amount of CO_2 given off, so the dependent variable is ordered (type 2). A table can now be constructed which effectively defines what must be done:

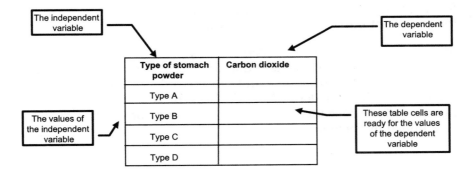

As the measurements are taken, they are inserted into the table cells. The order of collection in the case of categoric independent variables is often quite arbitrary e.g. the order in which the bottles of stomach powder happened to have been labelled:

Type of stomach powder	Carbon dioxide
Type A	Most
Type B	Least
Type C	None
Type D	Average

The data can be collected in any order, but when they are displayed in a table, it is easier to read if they are put in some kind of order. Usually this means redrawing the table, an easy enough task if it is in a spreadsheet. The order will depend on the question.

If the purpose of this exercise was simply to report the volumes of carbon dioxide produced by these carbonates, then it would be sensible to order them alphabetically by type as above so that the reader could easily locate a particular carbonate. But suppose the question is about which type of stomach powder produces the *greatest* volume of gas, the reader will be more interested in the order of volume of carbon dioxide produced and so it is sensible to put the types of stomach powder in either increasing (as below) or decreasing volume of carbon dioxide:

Type of stomach powder	Carbon dioxide
Type C	None
Type B	Least
Type D	Average
Type A	Most

5.2.2 Using and presenting a table with an ordered independent variable (types 4, 5 and 6)

Investigations in which the independent variable is ordered are similar. The data may be collected in that order or randomly. But the table of data should then be sorted either in the order of the independent variable or, where the dependent variable is ordered or continuous, in the order of the dependent variable. The preferred presentation will be determined by the question.

5.2.3 Using and presenting a table with a continuous independent variable (types 7, 8 and 9)

If the independent variable is continuous, the organisation of the table reveals a lot more information about the experiment. We shall use a typical school experiment to illustrate the point:

How does the bounce of a squash ball depend on the temperature of the ball?

The table, ready to receive the results, would look like this:

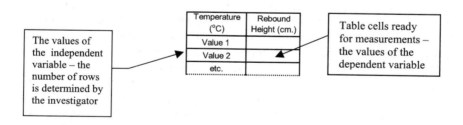

As discussed in the last chapter, the continuous independent variable (the temperature of the ball) can have any value within a range. The choice of the *number of values* selected by the investigator is reflected in the number of rows in the table. The *range* and the *interval* or gap between each reading is also shown in the table. In the next table you can see that the investigator has chosen 10 readings within the range 5–95 °C, at 10 °C intervals.

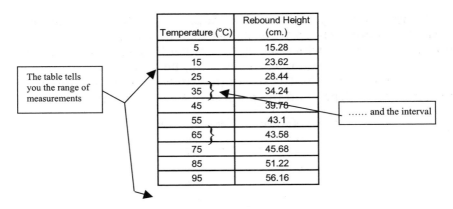

Temperature (°C)	Rebound Height (cm.)
5	15.28
15	23.62
25	28.44
35	34.24
45	39.78
55	43.1
65	43.58
75	45.68
85	51.22
95	56.16

The table tells you the range of measurements

...... and the interval

So, just by looking at a table with a continuous independent variable, we can see the range, interval and number of readings which the investigator is going to use in the experiment.

A note on presenting tables

In *intervention investigations,* if you are only reporting a small number of measurements, the table which was used to collect the raw data may suffice for a final report. However, if the number of readings is large, the table may become unmanageable and it then becomes more sensible to present a table summarising the data, making it easier for the reader. In the example that follows the data have been summarised using means.

Results of ten bounces at each temperature

Temperature (°C)	Mean rebound height (cm)
5	13.07
15	21.62
25	28.45
35	34.24
45	35.78
55	42.56
65	43.98
75	44.02
85	50.34
95	54.73

In *non-intervention investigations,* the investigator does not actively choose the values of the independent variable. There may not be any choice of the range, interval or number of measurements. Take the example of a study of birds in which data are collected on the weight of the eggs and the age of the mother. Supposing the age of the mother birds ranges from 6 to 25 years. Rather than present mean egg weight for each year of age, which would be a rather long table, the data can be summarised. For example, the ages can be grouped into bands as shown in the next table. The size of the bands is chosen by the investigator and will depend on the purpose of the investigation.

Age of mother (years)	Mean egg weight (g)
<10	300
10–15	350
16–20	400
21–25	450

It is often much easier to see trends or patterns when the data are sliced up into manageable 'chunks' like this. Notice one of the limitations of this table is that there is no indication of the number of cases in each category. Ideally this should be indicated in the table, for example, by using another column.

5.2.4 Some technical details

Tables have an agreed format. Here are some examples to illustrate the point:

A

Make of washing machine	Water capacity (litres)

B

Weight on plank (Newtons)	Sag from original position (cm)

C

Fertiliser type	Potatoes per acre (x1000)

Any column heading should have all the information needed to define the table's meaning. For a categoric variable, the heading involves only a description of the class of things from which the 'values' are drawn

– washing machines e.g. Hotpoint (example A). For a continuous variable, it must include the units (example B) and any multiplier (as in example C).

The aim is to make the entries in the table as parsimonious as possible – simple labels and/or numbers – thus ensuring that the data can be rapidly read and assimilated.

A title can also help to further clarify the meaning of the table, e.g. 'The water capacity of three different makes of washing machines tested in July 1997'.

5.3 Graphs

Graphs are another way of presenting and reporting data. It is nearly always easier to read, or see a pattern in, a graph than a table. We shall see in this section that line graphs can also be used to help determine the range and interval of the measurements of the independent variable. So, like tables, graphs have two purposes:

- as a tool *during* an experiment to help decide on the range and interval of measurements; and
- to display and report data *after* an experiment making it easier to see patterns and trends.

Graphs come in three basic varieties: line graphs, bar charts and histograms. Whatever the type of graph, it is good practice (but again this is only a convention) to put the independent variable on the x-axis and the dependent variable on the y-axis.

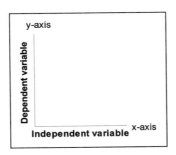

Quite often, the three types of graphs (line graphs, bar charts and histograms) are used interchangeably and often inappropriately. What are the criteria which determine which sort of graph is appropriate to a particular data set?

5.3.1 Which type of graph?

The combination of the types of the main variables in an experiment determines the most appropriate type of graph to use to present the findings. Consider again the nine combinations of variable types reproduced below. Where both the independent and dependent variables are non-numerical, a graph or chart is not appropriate: the data are best presented in the form of a table only. This applies to types 1, 2, 4 and 5 (shaded in the following table):

	Dependent variable		
Independent variable	Categoric	Ordered	Continuous
Categoric	1	2	3
Ordered	4	5	6
Continuous	7	8	9

We shall turn now to considering the most appropriate type of graph for the remaining combinations of variable types all of which involve continuous data.

5.3.2 Graphs for type 3 investigations (categoric–continuous)

The data stemming from an investigation like this are nominal because the independent variable is *categoric*. They are best displayed using a bar chart. For instance, the following chart shows data for the stomach powder investigation:

Type of stomach powder	Carbon dioxide (cm^3)
Type C	0
Type B	12
Type D	28
Type A	56

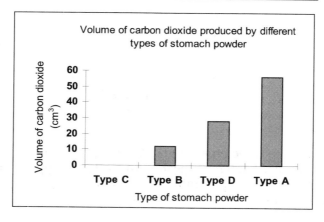

Because the independent variable is categoric, the four types of stomach powder are unrelated: they are simply names. There is no meaning to a point on the axis mid-way between Type B and Type D and it is only for convention's sake, and neatness, that the bars are drawn equally spaced. As in the presentation of results in the table, if we are interested in the magnitude of the volume of carbon dioxide produced, the bars are best arranged in order of increasing or decreasing volume.

5.3.3 Graphs for type 6 investigations (ordered–continuous)

The same type of graph, that is, a bar chart, is also the most appropriate for an investigation where the independent variable is ordered and the dependent variable is continuous. The reasoning is similar: although we now know the order of the amount of carbonate in the stomach powders, we cannot express this numerically so the positioning of the values on the x-axis is arbitrary, although usually evenly spaced for convention and neatness:

Amount of carbonate	Carbon dioxide (cm^3)
None (C)	0
Least (B)	12
Average (D)	28
Most (A)	56

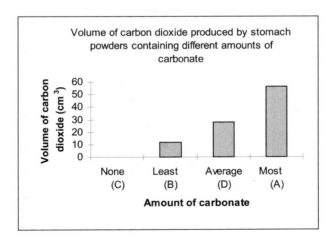

5.3.4 Graphs for type 9 investigations (continuous–continuous)

When the independent and dependent variables are both continuous, then the most appropriate type of graph to draw is a line graph. Take the example of a typical school physics practical investigating the extension (or stretch) of a spring with increasing loads as in the table and graph below. The spacing between the points on the x-axis is now much more important because the data for the independent variable (the load on the spring) are interval data. Each square on the graph paper represents a unit of measurement so that both axes behave like a ruler. There is only one place where each point can be correctly plotted because each point shows the actual extension with a particular load. Plotting all the measured points enables a line to be drawn and the overall pattern to be seen. The line then represents an infinite series of points, every one of which is just as real a value as the ones we chose to measure.

Load on spring (N)	Extension of spring (cm)
0	0
2	3
3	5
4	7
5	9
6	11
7	13
8	16.5
9	21
10	25

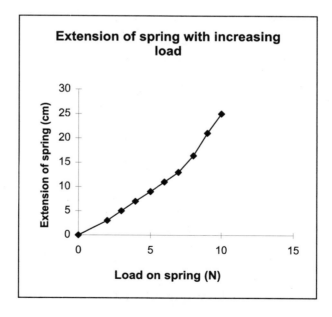

Look carefully at the way the following data have been plotted on the next line graph and see if you can spot a very common mistake:

Load on spring (N)	Extension of spring (cm)
0	0
3	5
4	7
5	9
8	16.5
10	25

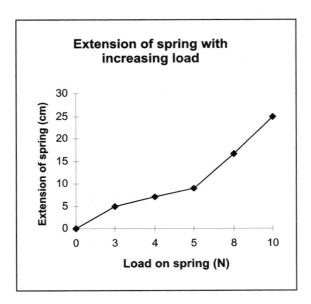

What you may have noticed is that the values of the independent variable have been treated as *categories,* as if the interval between them was meaningless (so that the space between 5 and 8 is the same as the space between 4 and 5). Notice too that because the data have been treated as categoric, the *shape* of the graph has changed. Plotting graphs incorrectly can therefore be very misleading.

The key difference between a bar chart and a line graph is that a line graph represents a numerical or mathematical relationship and thus has more 'buried' within it. As we saw in the last chapter, this is the strongest combination of independent and dependent variables in that there are two sets of interval data which provide considerable potential for exploring the underlying relationship. We shall explore the power of line graphs in more detail later in the book.

Using line graphs to determine the best range and interval of measurements.

In an investigation with a continuous independent variable, the number of values of the independent variable is infinite so that the investigator has to choose not only how many values to use but also which particular ones. In choosing these values, three decisions have to be made:

- What *range* should I choose – that is, which will be my highest measurement and which the lowest? (the spread of the values)
- What *interval* should I choose between my readings: for example, will it be 1 cm, 10 cm or 100 cm?
- How many measurements do I need to take altogether? – the *number* of readings

The *range* and *interval* determine the number of readings. Line graphs can be used during the experiment to help to make these decisions.

Sometimes the impression is given that there should always be six values of the independent variable for a line graph. This is not how it should be done. The better way to do it is:

- Take a smallish number of measurements, well spread out, and evenly spaced, to get a feel for what the relationship is like. (In other words, treat this as a trial run!)
- Plot your readings onto a line graph *as the data emerges* and examine the relationship. Are there any points at which the graph appears to flatten off or steepen or any other such change?
- If so, do some more measurements in that area to check on what is happening.
- Have the 'edges' of the relationship been tested – should the range be increased because something interesting might happen?
- If so, increase the range of the measurements until you are satisfied.

Note also that the *range* of readings will be determined in part by the purpose of the investigation. For example, if you are testing the sag of a diving board, it would be sensible to choose the range by finding out the weight of the lightest possible and heaviest possible divers who would be allowed to use the board. In school science, however, the same experiment might be done in a physics lesson where the purpose is to find out how a plank of wood (or 'diving board') behaves when loaded at its free end. With this approach, it is important to map out the relationship because we are seeking to generalise from this data to many sorts of planks and scenarios. So the choice of range is determined in part by the purpose and context of the investigation.

☆ ☆ ☆ ☆ ☆ ☆

Take a look at this example:

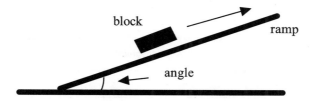

How does the force needed to pull a stone block up a ramp depend on the angle of the slope?

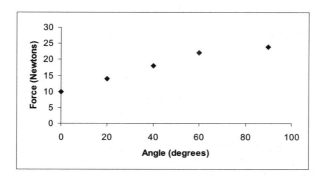

Trial 1

On the first trial run, five measurements were taken at angles of 0° (i.e. flat), 20°, 40°, 60° and 90°. The results were plotted straight onto a line graph:

The first part of the graph appears to be a straight line but the last part of the line does not follow the same pattern. The shape of the graph between these two points was unknown – it might be two straight lines so that the graph flattens off or plateaus or the line might continue to rise and then curve or turn over. These two possible shapes are shown on the next page:

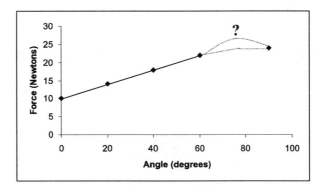

The students decided to take more measurements to explore the shape of the last part of the line between the two highest angles, 60° and 90°.

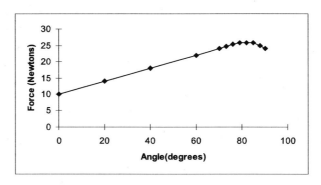

So in this example, the line graph was a guide to help to decide on the most appropriate interval and number of readings to reveal the full extent of the underlying relationship between force and the angle of the ramp.

☆ ☆ ☆ ☆ ☆ ☆

Graphing data in non-intervention investigations

In non-intervention (but also sometimes in lab-type) investigations, because the investigator does not actively choose the values of the independent variable, this often results in a large number of values of the independent and dependent variables. In this case, it is useful to plot a 'scattergraph' or 'scattergram' which is a form of line graph where the points tend to look as if they have been 'scattered' on the graph. Here is an example showing the relationship between the length and weight of a species of birds' eggs:

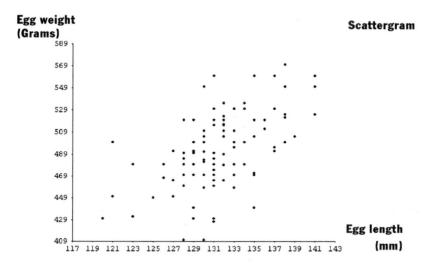

The graph shows that as the weight of the egg increases, its length also tends to increase. However, the graph is not a clear straight line and it would be quite difficult to decide where to draw a line (there are mathematical techniques to help). Nevertheless the scattergram serves its purpose of illustrating the shape of the data. This scattergram demonstrates a positive relationship or a positive *correlation*. It is called positive because the two variables change in the same direction (both tending to increase together). But of course the pattern of the data could be in the opposite direction, which is known as a negative correlation, as in the following graph which might be, for example, a graph of temperature and dissolving time:

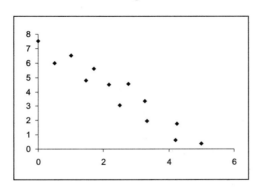

If there is no clear relationship between two continuous variables, then the correlation is weak. The weakest correlation of all is a 'zero correlation', illustrated below, which shows no relationship between the two variables.

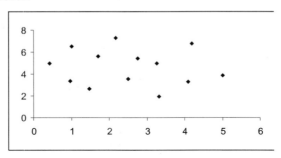

Correlations can be quantified using the correlation coefficient 'r'. The correlation coefficient has a range from +1 to –1. When r = 0, there is no correlation. When r = +1 or r = –1, then there is a perfect positive or negative correlation. The closer the correlation is to 0, the weaker it is. As a rule of thumb, a correlation of >0.7 is considered to be a strong correlation.

5.3.5 Graphs for type 7 and 8 investigations (continuous–categoric/ordered)

We are left with two types of investigations which both involve interval data in that the independent variable is continuous. We cannot envisage a sensible way of presenting continuous categoric data graphically in type 7 investigations, although it is possible to present type 8 investigations as follows:

Percentage of carbonate	Carbon dioxide
0	None
10	Least
25	Average
50	Most

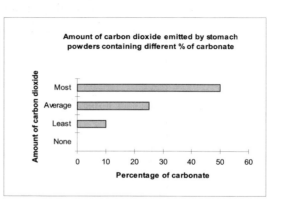

Since the dependent variable is ordered, it is best represented by a bar chart. To keep the convention of positioning the independent variable on the x-axis, the data are presented in a 'sideways' bar chart.

5.3.6 A note on the special case of a histogram

A histogram is not just a joined up bar chart! It should *not* be used for categoric data – a very common mistake. If you were to do so, it would imply that the categories joined up in some way. Nominal data is defined by the fact that the categories bear no obvious relation to each other and so a bar chart, not a histogram, is the most appropriate choice.

Consider the following data:

Height (cm)	Number of people
140–149	12
150–159	19
160–169	18
170–179	23
180–189	26
etc.	

Here the independent variable (height) is continuous but it has been grouped to show the pattern in the data better. This sort of data cannot be represented by a bar chart because the groups are related to each other, but a line graph is not appropriate either as the data is not that of a point, but a range. This sort of data is best represented in a histogram:

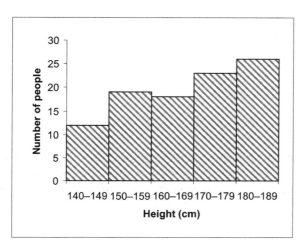

The bars of the histogram cannot be arbitrary in width or position: the width of the histogram bars must represent the range of values (10 cm in this case) and all be equally wide and contiguous. (Note: if the ranges are not all the same then the width of the bars *can* change – for instance, if the last row of data had been collected for 180–199, rather than 189, then the bar would be twice the width!)

5.3.7 Some technical details

Any graph should show the underlying structure of an investigation in terms of the independent and dependent variables (but not the control variables), the unit of measurement, the number of readings and, in the case of a continuous independent variable, also the range and interval of the readings.

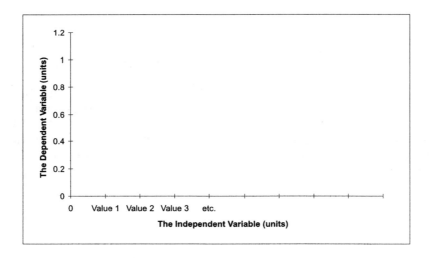

☆ ☆ ☆ ☆ ☆ ☆

Take a look at this example which is based on a glossy leaflet picked up in the sports section of a departmental store about 'Slimtone', an automatic exercise belt that you put around your waist which is supposed to tone up your stomach muscles:

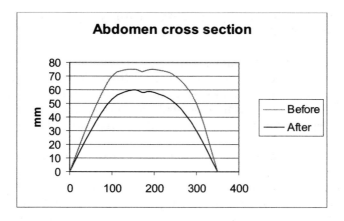

What does this graph tell you?

☆ ☆ ☆ ☆ ☆ ☆

You will probably find the graph difficult to understand, not least because the axes are not labelled properly. What is the y-axis? Is it the distance round somebody's stomach? Is it supposed to be a cross-section from the spine forwards? It is hard to make any sense of this graph. Attempts to 'blind' the public with this sort of scientific-looking nonsensical graphs are not uncommon. So, beware!

☆ ☆ ☆ ☆ ☆ ☆

5.4 Summary

This chapter has explored the use and presentation of tables and graphs and how they relate to the structure of investigations:

- A table can be used as an organiser before beginning practical work. The table shows the underlying structure of the intended investigation or experiment as shown below:

The **independent** variable (units, if continuous or grouped continuous)	The **dependent** variable (units)
Value 1	
Value 2	
Value 3	

- A table is also a way of recording measurements as they are made during the investigation and a way of displaying data after the investigation is complete, although it may have to be redrawn for example, so that the data are ordered. The table tells the reader the structure of the experiment in terms of the independent and dependent variables (but usually not the control variables), the unit of measurement, the number of readings and, in the case of continuous independent variables, also the range and interval of the readings.
- A graph is a way of reporting data and is usually easier to read than a table.
- A graph can be used during an experiment to plot continuous data *as it emerges* as a tool for optimising the range and the interval of the measurements so that the full pattern in a relationship can be explored and displayed.
- The type of graph is related closely to the type of data. For investigations with no numerical data, there is no sensible graph or chart: a table is the best way to report the data in these cases. For the most common combinations of variables involving continuous data, the following table summarises appropriate choices:

Independent variable	Dependent variable	Type of data	Type of graph
Categoric	Continuous	Nominal	Bar chart
Ordered	Continuous	Ordinal	Bar chart
Continuous	Continuous	Interval	Line graph

It is also possible to draw a sideways bar chart for investigations with a continuous independent variable and an ordered dependent variable (type 8).

- Incorrect plotting of line graphs can distort the shape of line graphs and lead to poor interpretation of the data.
- Histograms are used for grouped continuous data and should not be confused with bar charts.

5.5 Looking forward, looking back

It should be clear from the above that tables and graphs are not only ways of reporting and looking back at data which has already been collected. Tables are also tools for organising data in advance of the experiment (looking forward) and graphs are a means of getting a feel for the data as it emerges during the data collection period. Because you can tell a lot about the design of an investigation from a table or graph, then it follows that they are a means of exploring the validity of the design of an investigation. But remember that tables and graphs *do not tell you everything about the design*. They are both limited in the information that they give you. For example, usually tables and graphs do not show you which variables were controlled. In general, they also do not tell you anything about sample size or about the method of measurement.

So in *looking back*, supposing all you are shown is a table or a graph (which is often the case in press articles), there are a lot of questions you need to find answers to in order to find out about the validity and reliability of the investigation or experiment.

Another point when you look at graphs is that you should notice carefully how a graph has been plotted. We have seen how incorrect plotting can distort the shape of the graph. We shall see that this is important when we consider graphical interpretation. The scales on the axes of graphs can also be stretched or shrunk to emphasise one side of a relationship or to make a particular point which may not be justified. Again this 'trick' is very common in press reporting of science-related issues.

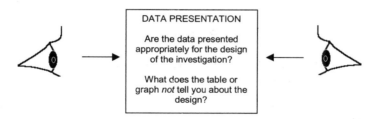

DATA PRESENTATION

Are the data presented appropriately for the design of the investigation?

What does the table or graph *not* tell you about the design?

You can add these points to your decision tree – an example follows on the next page.

Some of the examples in this chapter have shown that there is no fixed order for decision-making in investigations. Often 'fine-tuning' needs to be done by, for example, using the graph of ongoing measurements to go back and take more readings or looking at the results and deciding to repeat the investigation this time controlling another variable. Or you might decide that identifying a variable as continuous is necessary after all. This could be illustrated by adding arrows 'circling back' on the decision making tree.

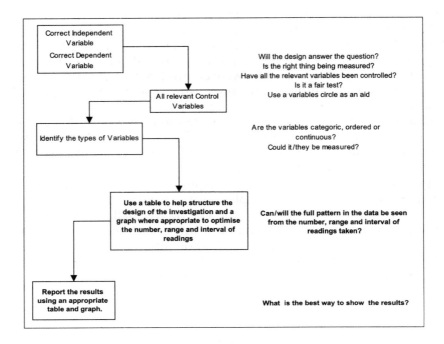

☆ ☆ ☆ ☆ ☆ ☆

Before you move on, take a look at this table based on one from a popular consumer magazine:

OUR FOOD TESTS - THE POOR RESULTS				
Airline	*To-from*	*Food*	*TVC (million)*	*E. COLI (million)*
Cold meals				
Europe Air	Gibraltar-Gatwick	Crab terrine	16	-
UK flier	Stansted-Glasgow	Beef	42	-
World Air	Heathrow-Athens	Turkey	14	-
World Air	Athens-Heathrow	Salmon	7.2	-
World Air	Athens-Heathrow	Chocolate gateau	15	0.0057
Hot meals				
Europe Air	Gibraltar-Gatwick	Meat and sauce	0.68	-
Wing Jet	Luton-Mahon	Meat and sauce	0.017	-
UK Hopper	Belfast-Heathrow	Sauté of prawn	0.005	-
UK Hopper	Belfast-Heathrow	Rice pilaf	0.006	-

Key: TVC= total viable count, i.e. number of bacteria per gram of food

Supposing you are a regular air traveller and have suffered from stomach upsets after airline meals. Jot down what else you need to know to be confident that the information in this table is valid.

Some of the other things you might want to know are *how many* meals of each kind were sampled, or *when* was the food was sampled (at the time it was eaten?), or what diagnostic tests were used to arrive at the figures? A lot more information is needed before you can decide, for instance, whether you should avoid the tempting chocolate gateau if you happen to fly with World Air.

Where are you?

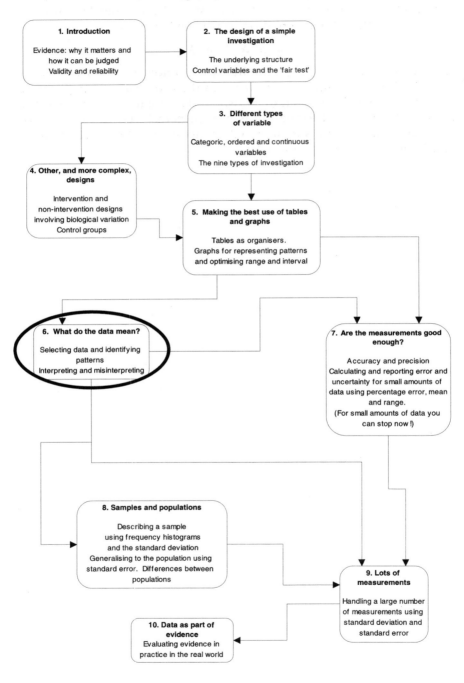

1. Introduction

Evidence: why it matters and how it can be judged
Validity and reliability

2. The design of a simple investigation

The underlying structure
Control variables and the 'fair test'

3. Different types of variable

Categoric, ordered and continuous variables
The nine types of investigation

4. Other, and more complex, designs

Intervention and non-intervention designs involving biological variation
Control groups

5. Making the best use of tables and graphs

Tables as organisers.
Graphs for representing patterns and optimising range and interval

6. What do the data mean?

Selecting data and identifying patterns
Interpreting and misinterpreting

7. Are the measurements good enough?

Accuracy and precision
Calculating and reporting error and uncertainty for small amounts of data using percentage error, mean and range.
(For small amounts of data you can stop now !)

8. Samples and populations

Describing a sample using frequency histograms and the standard deviation
Generalising to the population using standard error. Differences between populations

9. Lots of measurements

Handling a large number of measurements using standard deviation and standard error

10. Data as part of evidence

Evaluating evidence in practice in the real world

Chapter 6

What do the data mean?

Introduction

In the last chapter, we considered the best way of presenting data in tables and graphs and explored how the presentation relates to the design of the experiment or investigation. In this chapter, we will look at what tables (like the one in the headline below) and graphs tell the reader.

Health risk to women with new pill		
	New pill	Old pill
1996	30	15
1997	25	20
1998	28	18
1999	24	21

Making sense of data by interpreting tables and graphs, which is second nature to a scientist, can be problematic for people who use them rarely and not as an integral part of their 'language'. There are strategies to cope with even the most complex table or graph and they derive from an understanding of the use of tables in the design and data collection phase of an investigation which we explored in the previous chapters. Often, tables and graphs are seen as nothing more than a source of data from which to 'read' particular values; rather like a bus timetable. In fact there are several layers to what perhaps should be called reading, interpretation and analysis of such data. They are:

- the 'reading off' of particular data;
- the selection of sections of relevant data from complex data sets;
- the identification and interpretation of patterns within different types of data.

The skill of locating and reading off data points in simple tables and graphs is relatively straightforward so we will omit it here and move on to considering the selection of data from complex data sets.

6.1 Selecting data

6.1.1 Tables with multiple dependent variables

It is quite common for data in a table to represent the results of a series of experiments or investigations. The following three tables show the results of a series of investigations into physiological factors and their association with different types (and levels) of activity.

Identify the independent and dependent variable.

Activity	Breathing rate (breaths/min)
Sitting	17
Walking	21
Jogging	29
Running	51

Activity	Pulse rate (beats/min)
Sitting	66
Walking	79
Jogging	121
Running	161

Activity	Skin temperature (°C)
Sitting	34.3
Walking	34.5
Jogging	35.2
Running	36.8

☆ ☆ ☆ ☆ ☆ ☆

The independent variable is the activity and the dependent variables are breathing rate, pulse rate and skin temperature.

☆ ☆ ☆ ☆ ☆ ☆

These results could have been combined into a single table provided, of course, that the independent variable in the three investigations is not only the same but was investigated for the same values. In this case it was – each physiological factor was investigated for the same activities (sitting, walking, jogging and running). The composite table looks like this:

Activity	Breathing rate (breaths/min)	Pulse rate (beats/min)	Skin temperature (°C)
Sitting	17	66	34.3
Walking	21	79	34.5
Jogging	29	121	35.2
Running	51	161	36.8

Notice that the independent variable is in the left-hand column with the other three columns being the three dependent variables. Covering up any two of the columns 2, 3 or 4 of this table would select particular data sets and returns us to one of the three two-column tables on the previous page.

6.1.2 Tables with multiple independent variables

Consider the following hypothetical table. What is the variable structure here?

Airline Food type	Number of bacteria in 1 gram of food (million)					
	Summer			Winter		
	Hygena	Bugsline	Flyhigh	Hygena	Bugsline	Flyhigh
Turkey	13	19	7	9	13	5
Salmon	7	3	4	5	9	3
Crab	15	34	7	10	23	5
Chocolate cake	14	31	7	9	21	5
Beef	41	67	23	27	45	15

☆ ☆ ☆ ☆ ☆ ☆

There are *three* independent variables:

- the airline;
- the type of food;
- the time of year (summer/winter);

and one dependent variable:

- the number of bacteria

Compare that with the variables in the activity table in the last section where there was only one independent variable but three dependent variables.

☆ ☆ ☆ ☆ ☆ ☆

A table with multiple independent variables shows the *interaction* between these variables and so is often called a *cross-tabulation*. Any datum is at the intersection of two columns and therefore represents a particular value of each of the independent variables. Thus '13', in the top left-hand corner of the last table, is:

The number of bacteria	For	Air Hygena	and	Turkey
(the value of the dependent variable)		(the value 'Air Hygena' of the variable Airline)		(the value 'turkey' of the variable food type)

The table could be simplified or deconstructed into smaller ones. Try identifying the data you would put into a table of the number of bacteria in the food served by Hygena in the summer.

☆ ☆ ☆ ☆ ☆ ☆

Every data selection, whether of a single datum or a set in the form of a sub-table, should be accompanied by a statement as to the values of any variables in the table which have been excluded. So the simple table should state that the data are for 'Air Hygena' and 'summer'; two particular values of the variables Airline and Time of year. We have 'controlled for' these variables by the selection of bits of the table.

6.2 Identifying and interpreting patterns in different types of data and investigations

We saw in the last chapter that the nine types of combinations of key variables have their own associated formats for presentation of data in tables and graphs. The same framework can be applied to the *interpretation* of tables and graphs in secondary data. Rather than deal with all of the nine types, we will look at just some of them by way of exemplifying what can and cannot be deduced from data presented in these forms. The key questions which will guide us are:

- What do the data tell us? (Are there any patterns in the data?)
- What do the data *not* tell us that might invalidate our interpretation?
- Do the data suggest an association, a difference or a change between the variables?
- Can we use the pattern in the data to predict and generalise?*

*This includes an awareness of the limitations of the presentation of the data (i.e. What is missing? What does the table/graph *not* tell you?)

6.2.1 Type 1 tables (categoric–categoric)

Take a look at the next table:

Grass species	Recorded in area X
A	Yes
B	No
C	Yes

What do the data tell us?

We can say from this table that grass species A and C were recorded in area X and that species B was not.

What do the data not tell us that might invalidate an interpretation?

There is a lot the table does not tell us. For example, the table does not report how *much* of each grass species was growing in area X. Was there more of species A than species C? We do not know how often observations were recorded or what area each species covered.

In addition, as we noted in the last chapter, tables tell you little about the design of the investigation. So in the table above, notice that it does not tell us *how* the observation was done – for example, were sample areas examined? If so, how were the sample areas chosen?

This sort of data is usually presented in text rather than in a table. The reason for this is not surprising: in this form, the data tell you very little.

Do the data suggest an association, a difference or a change between the variables?

Because the data are categoric and there are no quantitative measurements, we cannot suggest an association between the independent and dependent variables.

Often data like this can serve as a starting point. For example, after collecting the above data, the investigator might then decide to take some measurements of the *quantity* of each species of grass (e.g. a measure of the area covered by each grass species). The investigation would then become a Type 3 investigation (categoric–continuous).

Can we use the pattern in the data to predict and generalise?

We cannot make any predictions from this sort of data. For example, we cannot predict whether other types of grass would be present in area X. Nor can we make any generalisation: the data are limited to that situation at that point in time.

6.2.2 Type 3 tables (categoric–continuous)

Suppose we are only interested in the *difference* between two values of the independent variable. Let us take the example of a new style contraceptive pill compared to an older one and the number of women taking the pill who develop deep vein thrombosis.

	New pill	Old pill
1996	30	15
1997	25	20
1998	28	18
1999	24	21

Figures: thrombotic episodes/100,000 women

What do the data tell us?
The table shows that there are more thrombotic episodes with the new pill than with the old contraceptive pill.

What do the data not tell us that might invalidate an interpretation?
The data do not tell us what the incidence of deep vein thrombosis is for women who are not on the pill. So there is no control group. There is also no indication of how the data were collected. For example, were the data taken from hospital records alone or from general practitioner records too? Were the records of all women on the pill in the UK examined or a sample? There is indeed a lot more information you would need to know but as we noted above, the associated text often provides more detail particularly about the design of the investigation.

Do the data suggest an association, a difference or a change between the variables?
The data suggest that there is a difference between the risk associated with the new and the old pill.

Can we use the pattern in the data to predict and generalise?
If we had sufficient information about the control group and the design, this data could be used to generalise about the risk of the new pill.

6.2.3 Type 6 (ordered–continuous)

Look again at the activity table in the last section, reproduced below:

Activity	Breathing rate (breaths/min)	Pulse rate (beats/min)	Skin temperature (°C)
Sitting	17	66	34.3
Walking	21	79	34.5
Jogging	29	121	
Running	51	161	

Note that the table has an ordered independent variable and three continuous dependent variables.

What do the data tell us?
Can you see any patterns or trends in the data?

☆ ☆ ☆ ☆ ☆ ☆

You will probably spot that there is an increase in the figures when you look *down* any of the numerical columns and also that the activities are ordered from sitting (low activity) to running (high activity). So the table as a whole tells us that:

• as the level of activity increases, breathing rate, pulse rate and skin temperature also increase.

Another point that you may notice by looking *across* the table is that:

• during the activity running, breathing and pulse rates increase significantly compared to jogging. Skin temperature on the other hand does not. (The biology of the situation tells you why – breathing and pulse rates rise, in part, to keep temperature down.) You can see these patterns by comparing the horizontal rows in the three columns. You will see that the increase in breathing and pulse rates from jogging to running is much higher than from sitting to walking or from walking to jogging.

The data in the table can be presented in a bar chart which helps to clarify patterns for the reader:

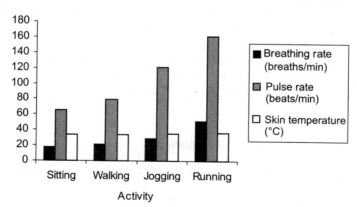

Notice that the bar chart makes it clear that skin temperature did not change much with the level of activity compared to the other two dependent variables. (You may already have spotted this in the table.)

What do the data <u>not</u> tell us that might invalidate an interpretation?

Although ordered data is more powerful than categoric data, it has inherent limitations. So in this example, we do not know exactly what the level of activities are. How fast were people walking, how fast were they jogging and running? Were they sitting passively or doing something that might increase their pulse rate?

In addition, the data as presented here do not tell us a lot of other things that might be relevant. For example, the reader does not know how many people were tested or how fit or how old they were.

Do the data suggest an association, a difference or a change between the variables?

From the data, it appears that there is some sort of an association between level of activity and breathing and pulse rates. But, from these data alone, it would not be wise to suggest any direct causal relationships. The data alone suggest several possible relationships, for example:

- increasing activity is associated with an increase in pulse rate;
- increasing activity is associated with an increase in breathing rate;
- breathing rate is associated with an increase in pulse rate.

To establish any causal relationship(s) would need further investigation.

Can we use the pattern in the data to predict and generalise?

Because the data are ordered, predictions are limited. However we can predict approximate breathing and pulse rates for the same person for another kind of activity such as skipping or sprinting if we put the levels of activity in order. Likewise if the breathing rate was low, e.g. 15 breaths/minute, we could predict that this person is likely to be in a state of low activity such as sitting or snoozing. But we cannot predict what the rates for walking to college would be for the same person because we have no quantitative measure of walking speed.

Although the data suggest an association between level of activity and breathing and pulse rates, without further information about, for example, sample size or measurement method (e.g. were the measurements taken once or repeated on more than one occasion for each person?) etc., we cannot generalise to other people or other situations. We need to know more about the validity of the design of the investigation or experiment and the reliability of the data collection.

6.2.4 Type 9 (continuous–continuous)

Speed (m/sec)	Stopping distance (m)
10	15
17	30
20	42
23	57
30	90

What do the data tell us?

This table tells you more than the previous one because both the independent and dependent variables are continuous. Here, we can pin down the relationship between the two variables more precisely because the variables are both measured quantitatively.

Again, a point graph helps the reader to get a feel for the overall shape of the relationship. Drawing a line on a point graph draws the reader's attention to the shape or pattern of the data:

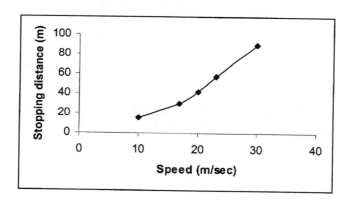

Think about what the graph tells you. What does it mean?

☆ ☆ ☆ ☆ ☆ ☆

The pattern here is very straightforward:

- as speed increases, stopping distance increases

You may also notice that:

- between 10 and 17m/sec, the stopping distance increases more slowly than at speeds of greater than 17m/sec.

What do the data **not** tell us that might invalidate an interpretation?

Although continuous data tell you a lot more than categoric or ordered data about the data itself, as we have noted before, a graph or table alone does *not* tell you about the details of the design such as the control variables or the measurement methods. So in the example here, we do not know the type or number of cars tested, or the road conditions, or how the stopping distance was measured (e.g. how accurate was it? Was the test done once at each speed or more than once?). Nor do we know what happens beyond the range of values given. Does the graph continue down in a straight line through the origin? What happens above 30 m/sec? Does it get steeper?

Do the data suggest an association, a difference or a change between the variables?

The table and the graph show that, above a minimum speed, there appears to be an association between speed and stopping distance. The association looks like a direct relationship: as speed increases, stopping distance increases, i.e. speed *causes* the car to take longer (and therefore further) to stop.

But a word of caution here: a point graph that suggests a straight-line relationship implies an association but *does not necessarily imply causality*. Consider again the scattergraph of the size of a species of bird eggs in the last chapter. A line of 'best fit' could be drawn through the data as shown:

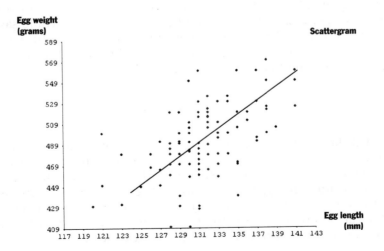

While egg weight and egg length are related, it would not be sensible to suggest that egg length *causes* egg weight or vice versa. But, if this was of interest, we might want to test other species of birds' eggs so that we could make a general statement about the positive relationship between the length and the weight of birds' eggs.

A correlation means that there is some kind of relationship between the two variables but it could well be a *chance* relationship or an *indirect* or *confounding* relationship so it should be treated with caution. There may be other variables 'intervening' in the relationship. For example, for people over 65, there may be a negative correlation between age and muscle power. It is probably not age that causes muscle strength to decrease but it is more likely that decreased mobility causes muscle wastage. So, if that is the case, then there is an indirect relationship between age and muscle power.

Can we use the pattern in the data to predict and generalise?

Returning to our speed/stopping distance example (pages 96–7), knowing this relationship enables us to make predictions for the same car under the same conditions. So, for example, if we knew that the same type of car in the same conditions was travelling at 25m/sec, we could predict the stopping distance by using the graph. What would you predict?

☆ ☆ ☆ ☆ ☆ ☆

Likewise if at the site of an accident, the marks on the road showed that the same car skidded for 100m before stopping, we could say that the driver was travelling at a speed of above 30m/sec. Continuous data can be powerful in this way, in that it enables prediction for values which were not measured.

☆ ☆ ☆ ☆ ☆ ☆

From this table and graph alone, we do not have enough information to generalise to other cars or other road conditions. If we had a lot more data so that we were satisfied that the experiment had sampled a range of different types of cars in a variety of road conditions and that the measurement method was reliable, then we could generalise to any car on any road. But the precise values will vary according to factors such as the type of car and the road conditions.

Interpreting other shapes of graphs of data from continuous–continuous investigations

(a) The line passes through the origin at an angle of 45°

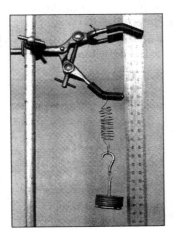

The graph and table below show data from an experiment in which a range of weights are hung on a spring and the increase (or *extension*) in the length of the spring is measured:

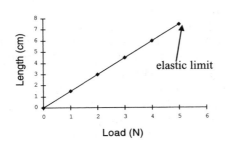

Load	Extension
(N)	(cm)
1	1.5
2	3
3	4.5
4	6
5	7.5

When the line of a line graph passes through the origin as in the graph above, then the relationship between the two variables is described mathematically as *directly proportional*. This means that as one value increases, the other increases in the same way. So if you look at the data in the table which was used for the graph, when the load doubles, for example, from 2N to 4N, so the extension of the spring doubles from 3 cm to 6 cm. This makes prediction of the extension for loads which have not been measured very easy indeed. Of course, there is a limit – if you put very heavy weights on the spring, you will damage the spring and it will exceed its 'elastic limit'. (You may know that there is a mathematical equation to describe the line: $y = mx$, where y = extension, m = gradient of the line and x = load)

(b) The line is straight but does not go through the origin

Here is another graph from the same experiment showing the *total length* (rather than the *increase* in length) of the spring with increasing load.

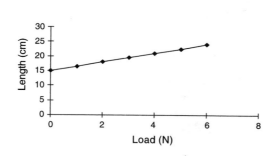

Load (N)	Length (cm)
0	15
1	16.5
2	18
3	19.5
4	21
5	22.5
6	24

Again, the table shows a regular increase in the spring's length, confirmed by the straight line through the data points. However, unlike in the last example, this time when the load is zero, the length (unlike the extension) is not zero. The relationship between the two variables is not directly proportional. The relationship can be described mathematically (you may recall the formula: $y = mx + c$, where y = length, m = gradient of the line, x = load and c = length with no load). Using the graph or the equation, predictions can be made for *any* weight or *any* length of spring, provided of course you do not damage the spring. So in this case, the interpretation is generalisable.

Indeed, it has been shown from repeated experiments with a lot of springs and with different types of spring, that the relationship between these variables (extension and load; length and load) is so predictable that it can be applied to almost all springs, whatever their thickness, diameter or length, although, of course, the values will be different for stronger or weaker springs. It is this widespread generalisability that resulted in the relationship being accorded the status of a *law*, and, as is often the case in science as elsewhere, the originator's name was attached to what is now known as 'Hooke's law'.

If a line can be described mathematically it is very useful because accurate predictions can be made without testing every value or every part of the line on the graph. Take, for example, the job of à civil engineer building a bridge. The engineer will rely on equations, albeit very complicated ones, for predicting how a metal girder will behave under given conditions. For example, will the girder (or girders) be strong enough to carry the volume of traffic which will pass over the bridge every day? To what extent will the metal expand on a hot summer's day? Questions like these can be answered from equations in conjunction with the data.

(c) Other shapes

There are, of course, many occasions when the relationship between two variables is much messier and where there is little or no predictability. Here are two examples in which the pattern is not a simple one. There is no simple, or even complex, single equation that will fit these relationships.

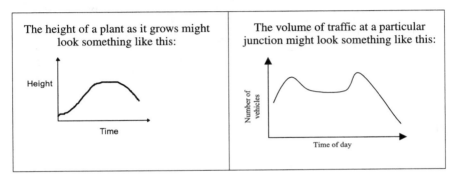

Consider the first graph. The relationship shown by the line in this line graph applies to a particular plant and will never be exactly repeated because no two individual plants and conditions will ever be precisely the same. When we speak of a pattern in this data, we are not seeing the pattern as an exact and regular relationship as in our previous examples, but rather as a trend over a given time period that might well be applicable to other plants. We can say that the plant makes a slow start, then has a major growth period followed by a period of stability. The mature plant then goes downhill as it dies! If we want to be more specific about, for instance, the growth of one type of plant, then we would need to collect data for many plants of the same type. We could then plot a graph of average height at given times and use the pattern to predict likely growth in any other plant of this type.

☆ ☆ ☆ ☆ ☆ ☆

Look at the second graph – what does it mean? Again we need more information to know whether or not the pattern would be repeated.

☆ ☆ ☆ ☆ ☆ ☆

Notice that we cannot predict with the same degree of accuracy for these relationships as we could for the spring/load relationship where mathematical modelling enabled accurate prediction and indeed, generalisation.

6.3 Some examples of interpreting and misinterpreting data

6.3.1 Drinking

This table shows the results of a survey asking young people whether they had drunk alcohol in the last week. The percentage of those who answered 'yes' are shown below.

Age (years)	1994		1996		1998		2000	
	Boys	Girls	Boys	Girls	Boys	Girls	Boys	Girls
11	8	4	7	6	4	2	5	5
12	10	9	12	9	14	6	11	9
13	22	16	27	22	16	14	18	19
14	34	26	37	35	28	29	34	31
15	52	48	50	55	48	40	52	46

(*Source*: http://www.ias.org.uk/factsheets/young.htm)

This is a complex table so it helps to work out the variable structure.

The independent variables are

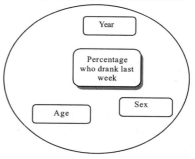

- age;
- sex;
- year;

and the dependent variable is

- percentage who drank last week.

We may need to select data depending on what we are interested in. Supposing you are interested in the difference between boys' and girls' drinking habits at different ages. We might then select the following figures:

Age (years)	Boys	Girls
11	4	2
12	14	6
13	16	14
14	28	29
15	48	40

Notice we have selected only the figures for 1998. We have controlled the variable, 'year'.

Supposing we are more interested in changes in young people's drinking habits over time. We might then select the data for boys for three years:

Age (years)	1994	1996	1998
11	8	7	4
12	10	12	14
13	22	27	16
14	34	37	28
15	52	50	48

We have controlled the variable, 'sex'.

What do the data tell us?
The data suggest lots of possible relationships in the large and small tables. For example, looking at the large table, if we were to average out the three years, it looks as if as age increases, so do the numbers of boys and girls who drink each week. Not surprising. The first small table tells us that among 11–15-year-olds, boys tend to drink more than girls. The second small table tells us that the trend for boys over time varies with age, e.g. at ages 11 and 15 drinking has declined over the three years while at age 12 it has increased.

What do the data not tell us that might invalidate the interpretation?
We do not know how many young people were asked at each age. We also do not know who asked them (this might influence the honesty of their reply – if it was the headteacher or one of their classmates). We also do not know how the question was asked – for example, did the question give examples of 'alcohol' – if so, were alcopops included?

Do the data suggest an association, a difference or a change between the variables?
There are several possibilities. For example, there may be an association between drinking habit and age and there may be a difference in boys' and girls' drinking habits in this age group.

Can we use the pattern in the data to predict and generalise?
We have already noted some of the information that is missing, such as sample size, which means that we must be cautious and limit the interpretation to the data. If we had more information and which,

confirmed the figures in the large table, then we could predict that boys are more likely to say yes to the question 'did you have an alcoholic drink last week?' than girls. We could generalise to the population as a whole (we will return to the issue of generalisation in Chapter 8). We could also generalise by saying that drinking is likely to increase with age from 11 to 15.

6.3.2 Two examples of misinterpretation

It is easy to overinterpret or misinterpret patterns in data. If you have a small sample, you may not be able to generalise to the population (see chapter 8). There are many examples of misinterpretation due to mistaking the type of association or, in other words, jumping to conclusions. Remember, *associations do not imply cause*. Here are two examples of misinterpretation:

Colds

A common misunderstanding is that a feeling of being cold, like when you get soaked in a snow storm, leads to catching a cold or going down with flu. But in fact, it is the cold or flu which causes you to feel shivery. So feeling shivery is a *consequence* of catching a cold and not a *cause*.

Drugs

In the 1950s, a consultant read about the affects of a new drug, known as DES, which was said to help women who had a history of stillbirths to produce live babies.

A patient, who had had two previous stillbirths, came to the consultant. He decided to give her DES. She produced a live baby. In a subsequent pregnancy under the care of the same consultant using DES, the woman produced a second live baby. When the woman became pregnant a fifth time, the doctor thought she might then be able to 'do it herself'. The baby was stillborn. Her sixth and last pregnancy was managed using DES and a live baby resulted.

It is tempting to conclude that DES results in live births in women with a history of stillbirths, i.e. a causal relationship. However, later, it was found that DES is ineffective and actually harmful, causing a variety of abnormalities including cancer in the women and children who had been exposed to it. The association between DES and live births had in fact been a *chance* association.

6.4 Summary

- Tables with multiple independent or dependent variables can provide a lot of information. They can be read by selecting and controlling factors to search for patterns in the data.
- Patterns in data in tables or graphs should be interpreted with caution: it is important to understand the limitations of the data and to consider alternative interpretations.
- The type of data (categoric, ordered or continuous) can limit the extent to which we can use the data to predict or generalise.
- It is also usually easier to detect a relationship (an association, a difference or a change) between two variables if at least one is continuous. But remember that *an association does not necessarily imply causality.*
- The shape of a graph can reveal a mathematical relationship which is very useful for accurate prediction.

6.5 Looking forward, looking back: interpreting the data

The interpretation of data in tables and graphs relates directly to validity. If the data have been interpreted incorrectly then any conclusions from the experiment is invalid.

In looking forward, the way in which you construct the design of your experiment or investigation will limit possible interpretations. For example, if you test male and female students' reaction times but do not record (or control) age, then your interpretation will be limited: you will not be able to say anything about whether age makes a difference. So your interpretation would say something about whether the sex of students relates to reaction times but it would have to state its limitations, e.g. the fact that age might make a difference. It might be that all the male students were older and that age rather than sex was associated with the pattern in the data.

Likewise in looking back, you should always ask yourself whether there are alternative interpretations of the pattern in the data. Might other factors be causing the pattern? Have the limitations of the data (or what the data do *not* tell you) been clearly identified? These considerations will affect how far we can generalise from the data.

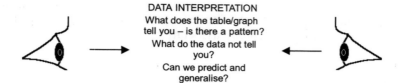

DATA INTERPRETATION
What does the table/graph
tell you – is there a pattern?
What do the data not tell
you?
Can we predict and
generalise?

We mentioned at the end of the last chapter that decision making is
not necessarily in the order implied by the arrows in the flowchart on
the next page. It is also not necessarily a one-off process. On some
occasions, once you have looked for a pattern in the data, you may
decide to repeat the experiment changing some aspects to improve it
and with the aim of clarifying the results.

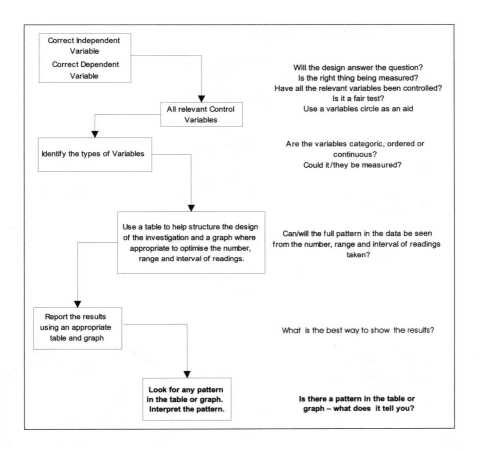

Where are you?

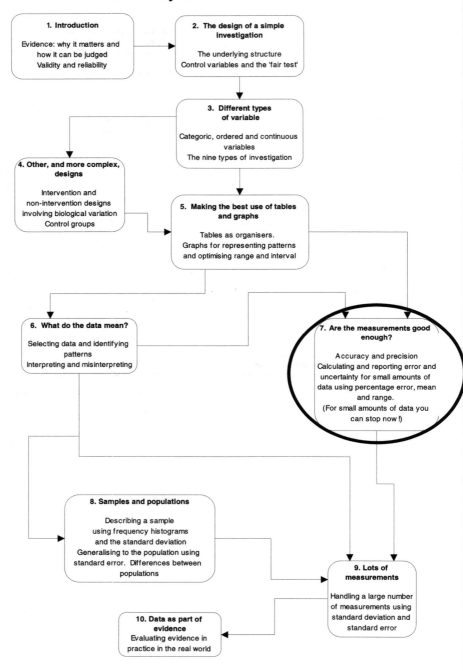

1. Introduction

Evidence: why it matters and how it can be judged
Validity and reliability

2. The design of a simple investigation

The underlying structure
Control variables and the 'fair test'

3. Different types of variable

Categoric, ordered and continuous variables
The nine types of investigation

4. Other, and more complex, designs

Intervention and non-intervention designs involving biological variation
Control groups

5. Making the best use of tables and graphs

Tables as organisers.
Graphs for representing patterns and optimising range and interval

6. What do the data mean?

Selecting data and identifying patterns
Interpreting and misinterpreting

7. Are the measurements good enough?

Accuracy and precision
Calculating and reporting error and uncertainty for small amounts of data using percentage error, mean and range.
(For small amounts of data you can stop now !)

8. Samples and populations

Describing a sample using frequency histograms and the standard deviation
Generalising to the population using standard error. Differences between populations

9. Lots of measurements

Handling a large number of measurements using standard deviation and standard error

10. Data as part of evidence
Evaluating evidence in practice in the real world

Chapter 7

Are the measurements good enough?

Introduction

So far we have considered the design of experiments or investigations and the presentation and interpretation of the resulting data. In the last chapter, we saw how continuous variables, which are defined by quantitative measurement, allow us to 'pin down' a relationship. Continuous variables can enable prediction, they have the potential to uncover causal or dependent relationships between variables and, with enough information, can allow an interpretation to be generalisable. In this chapter, we look more closely at the quantitative measurements associated with continuous variables in order to decide whether or not the measurements are reliable or good enough to answer the question.

There are many potential sources of error and uncertainty in making measurements. Here are the more obvious ones and ones which we shall explore in this chapter. Some of them are errors, some are uncertainties that are unavoidable:

Errors in making measurements

1. Human error – people make mistakes;
2. An instrument which is not zeroed for instance, or is badly calibrated, resulting in *systematic error*;

Uncertainties in making measurements

3. Reading the instrument scale itself can be difficult and may give an approximate or imprecise reading of the measurement;
4. The instrument may give different readings each time we use it – bathroom scales spring to mind!

5. Accuracy of the measurement process – a complicated measurement is prone to variation in the way it is carried out;

Uncertainties in the variable to be measured – uncontrolled variables

6. Uncontrolled variables may mean that the measurement of the variable varies from one measurement to the next, blood pressure for instance.

All these factors contribute to our judgement of the *reliability* of a measurement.

7.1 Errors in making measurements

7.1.1 Human error

Anybody can make a mistake in reading an instrument and staff in high-tech industries, where the instruments are complicated to read, often need to be trained to read them properly. But there are some basic rules to be learned.

• The most commonly known is the rule to avoid 'parallax error' – if the experimenter's eye is not directly in front of the pointer, the line of sight can cause an error in the reading, the size of which depends on the distance between the pointer and the scale. Next time you are in a car ask the driver and passenger to read the speedometer *from where they are sitting*!

• Another basic rule is to read the level of the *bottom* of the meniscus when you are measuring liquids (except for mercury).
• Make sure you read the scale or unmarked divisions properly – a lot of people find this difficult and it is a common cause of human error.

One way to check you are reading an instrument properly is to ask someone else who is perhaps more experienced to take a couple of readings and see if they get the same result.

7.1.2 Calibration and systematic error

Where does measurement begin?

We must begin this section with a little underpinning philosophy. When we wish to measure something in science we must have some sort of 'yardstick' (hence the origin of the term!) or standard unit. We have to define what we mean by a metre, or a second, or whatever. These definitions are the bedrock of quantitative science. What shall we choose to define as basic units?

The most fundamental units are those of *mass, length* and *time* (the kilogram, metre and second). They are defined in what might seem a rather curious way:

- *Mass* – the kilogram is defined as the mass of a piece of platinum-iridium alloy, chosen because it does not corrode. The standard piece is kept in a museum in France.
- *Length* – the metre was defined in relation to another piece of the same alloy in the shape of a rod and maintained at a constant temperature but, with more advanced technology, it is now defined as: *1 metre = length of path travelled by light in a vacuum during a time interval of 1/299792458 of a second.*
- *Time* – the second was derived from a fraction of a year although nowadays it is related to an atomic clock which is more constant than the length of the day or the year.

The principle of a measuring instrument

Once you have established a standard unit, you then have to make a practical measuring instrument. This involves 'calibration' – basically that means putting a scale on the instrument so that more than one unit can be measured.

If we consider length – it is not practical to carry around a 1 metre long platinum-iridium metal rod so instead we have wooden metre rules (and then other alternatives such as micrometers, or tape measures) that are exactly the same length as the rod. The metre rule is calibrated by dividing it up into 1000 equal parts to make a scale that allows for easier reading.

Many measuring instruments rely on *calibration*, that is, the marking of actual measured values of the quantity in question.

The purpose of calibration

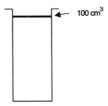

We will consider the calibration of a measuring cylinder. If water is poured into a straight sided vessel like the one in the diagram, there is a very simple relationship between the volume of the water in the vessel and the height up the side. In fact, they are directly proportional. A line graph would look like this:

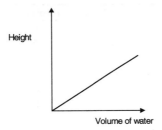

Because the relationship is linear, we can pour 100 cm³ of water into the vessel, mark the height, and then subdivide the intervening space. By the way, the linearity of the relationship relies completely on the uniformity of the cylinder. If it is not uniform, then the relationship is not linear and the calibration, which assumes it is, will result in the incorrect marking of the graduations.

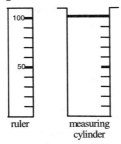

The calibration of the above measuring cylinder has been easy *because it is linear*. We only need the one calibrated value at the top for us to be able to subdivide the rest into equal divisions using a ruler.

But suppose the sides of the vessel, when highly magnified, looked like this:

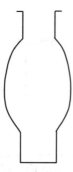

The first 10 cm³ say would go to a height of let us say 20 cm. The next 10 cm³ might go to a height of 30 cm. But the next 10 cm³ because the cylinder increases in width, would not go as high – it might only go to 35 cm.

Volume (cm³)	Height (cm)
0	0
10	20
20	30
30	35
40	40
50	45
60	55
70	65

(Approximations only)

What would the graph of height against volume look like?

Height of liquid in measuring cylinder

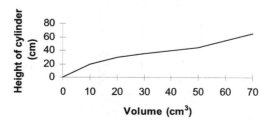

The calibration on the cylinder would have to reflect the pattern in this graph. If you did not know that the cylinder was not of uniform width, then you might divide it up into equal intervals. In that case, from 20 cm³ up the measurements would be wrong:

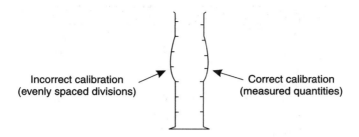

Incorrect calibration
(evenly spaced divisions)

Correct calibration
(measured quantities)

If you were calibrating this instrument for sale, then you would need to check the volume against a standard at various points. You can see that checking it only at 100 cm³ and then dividing it up would be no good. You would have to check it about every 10 cm³. Each measured value is a calibration point. A failure of calibration results in a *systematic error*. That is, a consistent error in one direction, not random around the 'true' value. Such an error is very difficult to spot – who checks a measuring cylinder to see if it is correctly calibrated? We tend to trust the manufacturers.

Two examples of calibration

All instruments have to be calibrated. They all have to be manufactured, and there is always some variation in any industrial production line. The details will of course differ from case to case. Two examples are given below by way of illustration.

(a) Thermometers: In reality, one of the main differences between a cheap and an expensive thermometer is the number of calibration points (that is, the number of points actually standardised). If you take a thermometer bought to measure the temperature of your greenhouse, it will probably only be calibrated at one point – e.g. 20°C. The typical school laboratory thermometer will have two calibration points – for example, a 0–100°C thermometer would be calibrated at 0°C and 100°C. Then there are thermometers with three calibration points – so they are divided into two halves and each is calibrated separately. Again in laboratory catalogues you will see more expensive thermometers with five calibration points where the scale has been calibrated in four portions. Five calibration points in a 100°C thermometer will give the required 0.1°C of accuracy which is required by BSI (British Standards Institute). If extremely high accuracy is needed, then thermometers with more calibration points will be used – for example a 5°C thermometer with a very large bulb might have 30 calibration points.

We thought it would be interesting to try out our own laboratory thermometers. So we did a quick test by putting a variety in some boiling water. Here are the results:

Type of thermometer	Reading in boiling water (°C)	Price (£)
Alcohol I	103	2
Alcohol II	104	2.50
Alcohol III	103	2
Mercury I	102	3
Mercury II	103	1.50
Digital I	100.7	35
Digital II	100.5	25

You can see that there is considerable variation and that the more expensive digital thermometers give measurements closer to the expected value. This does not mean that the cheaper thermometers are no good because they may read with consistent precision even if a little inaccurately. (We will return to the issue of accuracy and precision shortly.)

(b) *Measuring cylinders*: because calibration is critical, some measuring instruments are sold with a 'certificate of calibration' which provides the buyer with some reassurance that the gradations on an instrument are meaningful. The more calibration points there are, the more any non-uniformity in the measuring instrument can be mapped.

Notice in the example that follows about measuring cylinders adapted from a laboratory equipment supplier's catalogue that the certificate of calibration is stated as being measured at five points on the scale with volumes measured at 20 °C (because volume varies with temperature). The five points are spread out over the range (e.g. for the 100 ml measuring cylinder, the points would be at 20, 40, 60, 80 and 100 ml). It is only these points that have been calibrated.

Graduated cylinders, certified BS604			
With certificate of calibration which states the volume of distilled water at 20°C contained between zero and each of five points on the graduated scale.			
Capacity, ml	Graduations, ml	Pack quantity	£ per pack
5	0.1	2	25.84
10	0.2	2	25.84
25	0.5	2	27.50
50	1	2	27.68
100	1	2	30.66
250	2	2	40.78
500	5	2	55.94
1000	10	2	73.58
2000	20	each	55.67

7.2 Uncertainties in making measurements

In this section we shall look at the sources of uncertainty in using a measuring instrument to make measurements. We shall assume in what follows that there is no, or minimal, human error and that the measuring instruments have been correctly calibrated.

7.2.1 The uncertainty in the reading of the instrument → in reading pack.

Any instrument is limited by the smallest division that you/the operator can be expected to read. Let us suppose that the best we can read the divisions on a 15N forcemeter is to within 0.2 Newton. This is called the *reading error* (± 0.2 Newtons). Our best estimate for this error for any reading then is (measurement) ± 0.2 Newtons

For our 15 Newton forcemeter, 0.2 Newtons is going to be *relatively* more significant – that is a relatively larger error – at *lower* readings than at *higher* readings. If we calculate the percentage error this becomes clear:

15 ± 0.2 Newtons i.e. 14.8–15.2 Newtons – the % error is 1.4%
(0.2x100/15)

2± 0.2 Newtons i.e. 1.8 - 2.2 Newtons - the % error is 10% (0.2x100/2)

The percentage error over the range of an instrument would follow a graph something like this:

Force	Actual error	Percentage reading error
15	0.2	1.3
10	0.2	2.0
5	0.2	4.0
2	0.2	10.0
1	0.2	20.0
0.5	0.2	40.0
0.2	0.2	100.0

The closer the value is to the end of the scale (FSD) the less the percentage error. As the value drops close to zero, the error increases very quickly. It is this percentage error which really matters – the lower it is the better. That's why it's important to make a sensible choice of the right instrument for the task from a range of instruments with differing scales. Measurement experts talk about 'fitness for purpose', in other words, the right instrument for the job.

We now need to turn to problems with the inescapable fact that often measurements vary from one reading to the next. The measurement process can introduce uncertainty particularly if it is a complex one, such as in the measurement of blood pressure. We shall look at the consequences of this type of uncertainty through the ideas of *precision* and *accuracy*.

7.2.2 Precision – how precise are the measurements?

If we use the same instrument several times to take repeated measurements of the same thing, would we get exactly the same reading? The answer depends on the nature of the measurement but there is often some variation between repeated readings. Precision/imprecision (imprecision is often used in industry) is the variation between repeated readings or the degree of uncertainty about the reading. The variation between repeated readings is also traditionally known as 'random error' but because the variation is not really due to 'errors' or 'mistakes', it is now more commonly known as *uncertainty*.

> Precision is the variation between repeated readings

We can calculate the imprecision due to the measurement process in the following way:

Calculating the imprecision due to the measuring instrument
Imprecision can only be judged if the measurement is repeated a few times – if only to satisfy ourselves that the first measurement was not a fluke, or that the measurement procedure was faulty, or that we made a mistake in reading the scale. The more repeats that we can make, the more secure we feel that the average is 'good'.

Consider the following. The largest measurement you can make using an instrument is called its Full Scale Deflection, FSD. Suppose we are using a forcemeter which goes up to 15 Newtons FSD.

We take repeated measurements of the *same* force and get these results:

Measurement	Value
1	10.1
2	9.8
3	9.9
4	10.2
5	10.0
Average	10
Range	9.8–10.2

Variations in readings on a forcemeter could be due to any number of reasons. Ideally and depending on the significance of the measurement, we would take many more readings of the same force. If we only have a few readings, we can use the *range* as an approximation. The range here is from 9.8-10.2. The precision can be stated by reporting the average (10N) and the range as follows:

$$10 \pm 0.2 \text{ Newtons.}$$

If the precision of the measurement is crucial, then more readings of the same force should be taken and appropriate statistics, such as 'standard deviation' or the 'coefficient of variation', used to calculate and report the precision. We shall return to these statistical issues in chapters 8 and 9.

7.2.3 Accuracy – how accurate is the instrument?

When we talk about the accuracy of an instrument we are talking about how close the reading on the instrument is to the *true* value (one obtained very, very carefully indeed and checked against other instruments – even then there will be some uncertainty but we shall ignore that for now).

Accuracy is the closeness of a measurement to the true value

Precision and *accuracy* are fundamental to all measurements and underpin reliability. Their relationship will lead us to a better understanding of systematic error.

7.2.4 The relationship between accuracy and precision

Supposing we want to check four different weighing instruments with a weight which we are sure (by comparison with a standard) is 100g. Imagine that the four large dartboard-like circles below represent the readings we get from the four different weighing instruments. The bullseye is the 'right' answer, i.e. 100g and anywhere outside that represents mistake, error or uncertainty. The true reading is in the centre of the bullseye. The crosses represent repeated readings of the same measurement.

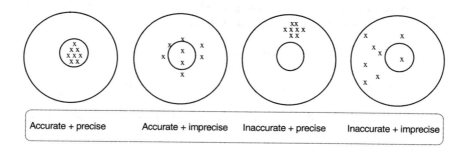

Accurate + precise   Accurate + imprecise   Inaccurate + precise   Inaccurate + imprecise

The first instrument (the first circle) is the best quality measuring instrument (and probably the most expensive) because all the repeated readings are very close to the true value (accurate) and the variation between the readings is small – it has good precision. A histogram of the frequency of repeated measurements from such an instrument would look something like this:

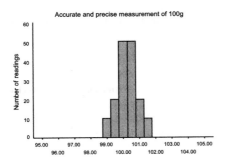

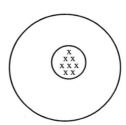

Accurate and precise

You can see that the readings are all clustered around the true value of 100g and that the range is from 99g to 101.5g so that, by using this instrument, you can be confident of getting a good reading. At the most, it will only be out by 1.5g.

The second instrument (the second circle) is not quite so good. Its accuracy is OK in that most of the readings are not too far from the true value but they are not very precise – when you repeat a reading it varies quite a lot. We can see this in the next histogram. Notice that the measurements range from 98 to 102.5g so that your measurement could be out by 2.5g.

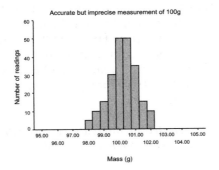

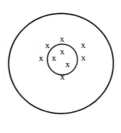

Accurate and imprecise

The third instrument (the third circle) is precise because all the readings are close together but they are not near the true reading, so its accuracy is poor. This instrument has, what is known as, a 'systematic error' or bias. If we know the relationship between the reading on this instrument and the true reading (i.e. we know the extent of the systematic error), then the lack of accuracy may not matter because the bias from the true reading might be predictable. We encountered systematic error in the section on calibration. Here we can see its effects.

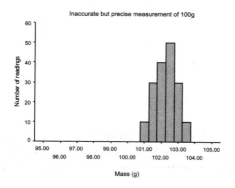

Inaccurate and precise

A note on systematic error

If the instrument is 100% accurate i.e. it gives you the true value, then there is no systematic error or no bias. Systematic error is possibly the most difficult type of error to spot because it is only by checking against a reference or standard, that you know to be correct, that you can detect it. In practice, in working laboratories for instance, companies will buy an instrument with stated accuracy conforming to known standards (e.g. national [BS, British Standard], international [ISO, International Standard Organisation] or US [ASTMS] standards) which guarantees a specified degree of accuracy and precision. Even then, it is wise to check periodically against a standard because wear and tear on an instrument can affect its accuracy. For example for thermometers, BSI recommends that:

It is desirable that thermometers be retested at intervals not exceeding five years, or more frequently if determinations at a reference point indicate that a retest is required.

In a report where measurement is particularly critical, then the manufacturer of the instruments may be specified in the report. The manufacturer in turn will also be subject to regular calibration checks. This particularly applies to balances. Consider the following case of systematic error based on a press article:

Semtex Blunder casts doubt on IRA bomb cases

The convictions in at least 12 IRA bombing cases were placed in doubt last night after the Home Office disclosed that equipment used to test for traces of explosives was contaminated. The contamination involved a component of Semtex (RDX). Minute quantities of RDX were discovered by accident two months ago in machinery used to analyse evidence in bomb cases at the Government's Forensic Explosives Laboratory in Kent. A small rubber plug on which test tubes are placed in a centrifuge holder (a machine used to spin liquid samples in test tubes at high speeds) was found to have absorbed tiny amounts of RDX. It was probably already contaminated when the machine was bought second-hand in 1989.

The contamination was discovered by accident when a technician broke a tube containing a control sample and the contents, which should have been uncontaminated, flowed onto the rubber plug. The technician carried on with the test which revealed a small trace of RDX in the sample leading to the suspicion that the rubber plug was contaminated.

Although regular checks were made of work surfaces and floors in the laboratory as a guard against contamination, experts admitted last night that it had never been thought necessary to test the equipment itself. One said: 'The requirement to do this particular thing was not very obvious. It was not spotted by either ourselves or by scientists representing defendants who have been in on dozens of occasions to check our work. Nobody thought of it.'[1]

Instrument 4 (the last circle) clearly is not much use at all – it is inaccurate *and* imprecise.

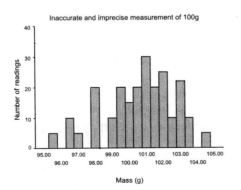

Inaccurate and imprecise measurement of 100g

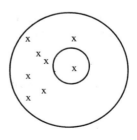

Inaccurate and imprecise

[1] P. Johnston, IRA bomb cases cast into doubt. Electronic Telegraph 15/5/96.

7.2.5 Accuracy of the measurement process – Round Robins

A 'round robin' is the name given to an exercise in which a central external agency sends a sample of the same substance to different laboratories and asks them to measure it (or something in it). The results of the different laboratories are then checked one against another. Round robins are often used when accurate measurement is critical, as in blood tests for example, and when measurement techniques are complex.

An example of a round robin is in the measurement of a substance in the blood called thyroxine (or T4), which is a hormone formed in the thyroid gland. An example of the results using nine different laboratory methods is shown in the graph below. Look carefully at these results and decide which method is the most inaccurate.

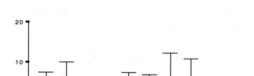

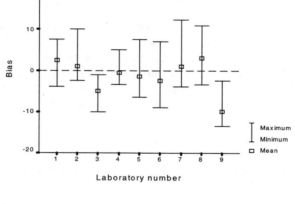

Methods 3 and 9 have the most inaccurate results. Method 9 shows a clear systematic error.

7.2.6   Some examples of indirect measurement processes

So far we have looked at relatively straightforward measurement processes using instruments that are readily available and in common use such as thermometers, measuring cylinders and forcemeters. You only get the quality that you pay for, but in general such instruments are reasonably trustworthy because the errors and uncertainties we have described here have been minimised in the design process. But sometimes the measurement process is far less straightforward and indirect indicators are used instead. Below are two examples.

Lichen as a measure of pollution

Some measurements are particularly difficult and expensive to make. How do you set about measuring the pollution in the air for instance? A well-known indicator which serves as an indirect measurement of pollution is the presence and abundance of lichens on stones. Lichens are very sensitive to pollution and are easily damaged or killed. Their presence is associated with clean air. How can we use lichens as a measuring instrument? Here are the steps in the process we would need to go through if lichens were to be used as an instrument rather than as an on/off indicator.

- Define what type of pollution is likely to be present. We shall suppose for this exercise that there is only one pollutant – acid rain.
- Grow samples of a species of lichen under varying conditions of acid rain to establish the level at which there is a noticeable effect (the sensitivity threshold of the instrument) and the level at which all the lichen dies (the full scale deflection of the instrument).
- Look at the lichen at various levels of pollution and establish whether, for instance, the mass of the plant/cm^2, or the area covered is the most sensitive factor to changing levels of pollution.
- Having decided on the best measure, plot a line graph (a calibration curve) showing how the factor varies with pollution level.
- Monitor the lichen growth in the real situation and use the calibration graph to get a measurement of pollution.

There are clearly many possibilities for errors to creep in here. What sample size of lichen is needed to be a clear indicator of a level of pollution? What we have here is a very imprecise instrument but one which is probably much less complicated than if we were to try to measure pollution by chemical analysis. It also has the advantage of occurring naturally so we can get estimates of pollution just by looking around.

The measurement of hormones in blood

A biotechnology company uses a technique called immunoassay to develop and manufacture medical test kits that are used in hospital and research laboratories in the measurement of picogram quantities (1 million-millionth of a gram) of hormone in a single drop of blood or serum. If a doctor needs to know the level of a particular hormone in the blood of a patient, the hospital laboratory could use one of these test kits to provide the answer.

Immunoassay relies on the ability of a specific antibody, or a mixture of antibodies, to detect and bind to minute quantities of the hormone, a reaction which is both highly sensitive and specific. The degree of binding can then be determined and the result quantified and expressed as the blood or serum concentration. So the level of hormone in the blood is determined indirectly by measuring the degree of binding of the antibodies.

7.3 Some rules for selecting instruments

We can now make up some rough and ready rules for selecting and using instruments.

1. Use any suitable instrument to hand to make a rough measurement of the quantity.
2. Choose an instrument for which your measurements are likely to be distributed towards the top of the scale. Remember the idea of 'fitness for purpose'.
3. Decide whether the instrument gives you the accuracy and precision you need.
4. Select an instrument with a clearly marked scale.
5. Have someone else check a measurement to make sure that you are reading the instrument properly.
6. Check, and adjust if possible, the zero of the instrument.
7. Check, if possible, the highest point on the scale (the full scale deflection) and several other points on the scale against a high quality instrument.
8. Repeat a reading a few times to get a feel for the repeatability of any measurement before you decide.
9. Repeat a reading with another instrument, if possible, to check for systematic error.
10. If an indirect measurement is a more viable method, then careful calibration will be necessary and there is likely to be a greater degree of uncertainty.

7.4 Uncertainties in the variable to be measured – uncontrolled variables

No matter how careful we are, a squash ball will never bounce to exactly the same height, a wire will never break at exactly the same force. There will always be some variable that has changed slightly from one reading to another – a draft in the room, bouncing on a 'hard spot' of the ball, variation in wire thickness for instance. This sort of uncertainty is different in principle from that we have discussed before. Earlier sections of this chapter were concerned with the variation in measurements due to instruments and human fallibility. But there was a goal – albeit unrealistic – of a perfect measurement. But the fact that a wire breaks at different forces depending on which bit of wire you choose is a fact of life – there is no 'right' answer. There is a range of right answers. The average tells you the most probable breaking force, and the range tells you how much any one instance might differ from that average. The important issue, then, is to repeat the measurement and, as a minimum:

- report the average of the reading
- report the range over which the readings will be spread.

This gives the reader (of the report) a 'feel' for what is likely to happen. If there is time and opportunity to take a lot of measurements, then there are better ways of reporting uncertainty which we will explore in the following two chapters.

7.5 Case study of blood pressure measurement

Let us pull all these ideas about error and uncertainty in measurement together by taking a particular example – the measurement of blood pressure.

If you have ever had your blood pressure (BP) measured by a doctor or nurse, the traditional method is for the doctor or nurse to wind a cuff around your upper arm, pump it up and then listen with a stethoscope (which just magnifies the sound) while watching a tube of mercury. This instrument (the mercury tube and the cuff) is known as a 'sphygmomanometer'. (Alternative electronic instruments for measuring blood pressure are now available but the accuracy and reliability, at least of the early versions, has been questioned.)

The sphygmomanometer allows the doctor (or nurse) to measure the pressure at which your heart is pumping blood round your body. The pressure in the artery in the arm (the brachial artery) is used for BP measurement because the pressure there is nearly the same as the pressure at the outlet from the heart. Two pressures are measured: the 'systolic' and the 'diastolic' pressure.

First, the doctor or nurse listens for your heart beat and then inflates the cuff, which is like a balloon, until the sound disappears and then continues to inflate the cuff for 30 mmHg above this level. The cuff is then slowly deflated at the rate of about 2 mmHg/s. The highest pressure at which the sound reappears is recorded – this is the systolic pressure. The sound becomes muffled and then disappears. The pressure at which the sound disappears is also recorded – this is the diastolic pressure.

This measurement process has many possible sources of error and uncertainty. Here are some:

Errors in making measurements

Human error:

- The cuff size may be wrong. A survey showed that 96 per cent of doctors regularly use a cuff size which is too small[2]. Measurement errors tend to be smaller with the larger cuffs.
- The doctor may listen for the wrong sounds.
- The doctor may not have good hearing.
- Measurements taken on three separate occasions over at least four weeks (recommended) may be taken by different nurses or doctors which can cause error if, for example, any one of these is listening for the wrong sounds or rounding up or down in a different way.

Calibration:

- The sphygmomanometer may not have been checked regularly – although the mercury may be reliable the rubber tube, valve and the other bits and pieces can cause problems. (The error here could be intermittent or it could be systemic error.)

Uncertainties in making measurements

Reading the scale

- The doctor may round up or down to the nearest 5 mm or even to the nearest 10 mm.

The measurement process

- The patient may not be in the right position – they should be sitting, not lying or standing.
- The patient's arm may not be in the right position – it should be kept at heart level.
- The patient may have just been drinking coffee or smoking – this can raise the blood pressure.
- The patient may have just been taking vigorous exercise which can decrease the blood pressure for several hours afterwards.

[2] Pickering T.G. 1994 Blood pressure measurement and detection of hypertension. The Lancet 344 31–35

- If the patient is talking, this can also raise BP.

And an example of systemic error:

- Some patients get anxious particularly if a doctor takes their blood pressure. This anxiety can cause the blood pressure to rise. This effect is known as 'white coat hypertension' – that is, raised blood pressure due to the presence of a doctor. (Having a nurse or technician take blood pressure has been shown to lessen this effect – the measurement taken is likely to be closer to the patient's daytime average than if taken by a doctor.)

Uncertainties in the variable to be measured

- The doctor may only take the measurement on one occasion, taking no account of variation which can occur from day to day even when all the obvious causes of blood pressure noted above are taken into account.

Accurate and precise blood pressure measurement matters. Most measurements are carried out because of concerns about suspected cardiovascular disease. Decisions as to whether to treat or not hinge on changes in blood pressure which depend on reliable and valid measurement. An article published in 1999 in the *British Journal of General Practice* reports that:

> as many as 30% of cases of mild to moderate hypertension are thought to be misdiagnosed by observer error. Up to a further 20% of those on treatment have sustained white coat hypertension and, unless they have other cardiovascular risk factors, they do not need medication.[3]

7.6 Errors and uncertainties in an investigation

It is only when a measurement is set in the context of a task, that we can decide whether a measurement is 'good enough'. How much uncertainty and error (e.g. reading error) you can accept, depends on the task, or the question you are seeking to answer. Again, this is the idea of 'fitness for purpose' – is the measurement good enough for this particular task? This is where judgement comes into play. Think about the bouncing of a ball and its uncertainty as a simple example. Suppose you were asked to find out whether five blue spot squash balls

[3] Aylett, M. (1999) 'Pressure for change: unresolved issues in BP measurement', *British Journal of General Practice*, (1999), 49: 136–9.

are the same in terms of their bounciness. You decide to drop each ball from a height of 1 metre and measure the first bounce or rebound. You have access to some sophisticated electronic equipment for measuring the height of the first bounce. Here are the results of three repeated measurements for each ball:

	Bounce height (cm)		
	Bounce 1	Bounce 2	Bounce 3
Blue ball 1	36	43	38
Blue ball 2	49	48	44
Blue ball 3	45	51	48
Blue ball 4	45	52	48
Blue ball 5	53	47	57

You can see in the table that the bounce heights vary considerably so that the random variation, or the uncertainty associated with the variable bounce height, is quite large. The measuring equipment means that the uncertainty associated with the measurement itself is small and calculated as ±0.2 cm. The uncertainty associated with the measurement is very small compared to the random variation in the bounce heights. So a sensible decision would be to ignore the instrument error.

The most common way to report the random variation (or imprecision) in a small amount of data is to state the mean and the range of the readings, indicating the number of repeated measurements:

Results for 3 bounces of blue spot squash balls

	Mean bounce height (cm) [range]
Blue ball 1	39.0 [36–43]
Blue ball 2	47.0 [44–49]
Blue ball 3	48.0 [45–51]
Blue ball 4	48.3 [45–52]
Blue ball 5	52.3 [47–57]

Or you could plot the results on a graph using vertical bars to show the range like this:

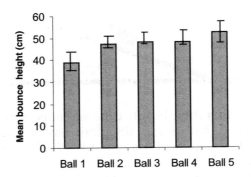

If the variation is greater than the measurement uncertainty, then we are reporting a real variation. In an investigation like the one just described, it is reasonable to be more concerned about the uncertainty associated with the variable, i.e. the bounce height, than with the instrument error which is relatively small. The key to this particular question (are the 5 balls the same?) of course is whether the variation in bounce height for any one of the balls is greater than the variation between the different balls.

☆ ☆ ☆ ☆ ☆ ☆

How would you interpret this data? Do you think the five balls are the same or not?

☆ ☆ ☆ ☆ ☆ ☆

Blue balls 2, 3 and 4 bounced to about the same height and on the chart they look quite similar. Ball 1 is clearly different, bouncing consistently lower than balls 2, 3, 4 or 5. It is difficult to decide whether or not blue ball 5 is different – more bounces would help us to find the answer.

☆ ☆ ☆ ☆ ☆ ☆

So in this example, it would be sensible to decide that the measuring instrument is good enough but the uncertainty in the variable itself (the bounce) means that more measurements may need to be taken to answer the question.

Compare the above with the following example, an experiment we met before in Chapter 5:

> How does the force needed to pull a stone block up a ramp depend on the angle of the slope?

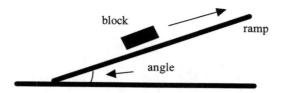

We shall assume that there is only time and opportunity to make three measurements and that we will, therefore, have to estimate the uncertainty of those readings. First, we might try the force needed when the slope is at zero and when it is near 90° to give us some sort of feel for the quantities involved. The force at 90° turns out to be about 8/9N and when horizontal about 3/4N. At intermediate angles we can expect some sort of smooth trend between those values, as in the following table:

Angle (degrees)	Force (Newtons)			
	Reading 1	Reading 2	Reading 3	Average
0	3.5	3.3	3.6	3.47
20	4.9	4.6	4.9	4.80
40	6.3	6.1	6.4	6.27
60	7.7	7.8	7.9	7.80
70	8.4	8.6	8.3	8.43
75	8.8	8.8	8.7	8.77
80	9.0	9	9.2	9.07
85	9.1	9.1	9.2	9.12
90	8.4	8.6	8.5	8.50

Let us concentrate on just one angle – say 60°. Suppose we take another two readings and get these results:

Angle (degrees)	Force (N)					
	Reading 1	Reading 2	Reading 3	Reading 4	Reading 5	Average
60	7.7	7.8	7.9	7.6	7.5	7.7

The instrument error has been calculated as ± 0.5N. So on the basis of instrument error only, we would expect the readings to fall within 0.5N either side of 7.7: between 7.2 and 8.2N. They do. Which suggests that the instrument error is greater than any random variation and so, in this instance, we do not need to worry too much about the uncertainty associated with the variable (unlike in the bouncing ball example). In this example, it is more important to report the instrument error.

There are various ways of combining errors in investigations or experiments where there is more than one measurement but we will not complicate the issues we are exploring here by getting into detailed mathematics. The reader who wants to know more about these techniques is advised to consult appropriate textbooks. A quick rule of thumb, however, is to add the percentage errors resulting from each and every measurement associated with one value of the variable. In the example above, the % error for reading the angle of the slope is added to the % error for the forcemeter for each angle separately.

You will have noticed the approximations in the calculations of error. It is important to realise that the percentage error is only an estimate and need not be calculated to many significant figures in most cases. Errors should not be treated purely mathematically. They are no more than an estimate and should correspond to common sense and be appropriate for the purpose of the experiment.

7.7 Summary

In this chapter we have explored some of the errors (e.g. human error, systematic error) and uncertainties (e.g. imprecision) associated with measurement. There can be error and uncertainty in the measuring instrument, in the measurement process and in the variable that is being measured. In considering, or in reporting any measurement, knowing its accuracy and precision allows us to decide whether it is good enough, or reliable enough, for its purpose. The level of error and uncertainty which is acceptable depends on the context of the task for which the measurement is required. In critically evaluating data, an awareness of uncertainty which is likely to be significant but is not reported may lead to the results being disregarded.

7.8 Looking forward, looking back

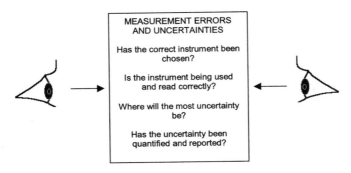

MEASUREMENT ERRORS AND UNCERTAINTIES

Has the correct instrument been chosen?

Is the instrument being used and read correctly?

Where will the most uncertainty be?

Has the uncertainty been quantified and reported?

In planning and carrying out your experiment or investigation, it is important to choose the most appropriate instrument for the task which will result in the required accuracy and precision. It is also important to check that the measuring instrument is being used and read correctly. Looking back at other investigations, you should look carefully for details of the measurement procedure. Do the experimenters report what instruments were used? Remember that systematic error is not uncommon.

Any report of an experiment should consider where the most uncertainty is likely to be and quantify and report significant uncertainty in the ways described in this chapter. Errors and uncertainties clearly affect the *reliability* of the data and the weight you can put on the evidence. For instance, if you know that there is a lot of random variation in a measurement, then you will want to know the size of the uncertainty so that you can decide how much weight to place on the evidence.

In considering the *validity* of a measurement we need to take a wider look as to whether we are measuring the right thing. Look back for example to the 'Lead in your Tea?' article in Chapter 2 or the following article:

> The Diane Modahl case, in which the athlete was wrongly accused of taking drugs to enhance her performance, was a classic case of a measurement which was disputed. It was about how the sample was taken, then handled, how stored, how things were extracted from it, as well as the measurement itself. Scientists get very excited about the instrument, about the bit of kit that does the final measurement. But sometimes the most important thing is how the sample was taken and stored. In this case, the consequences for the athlete were very serious – her livelihood depended on the validity of the data and it was invalid.

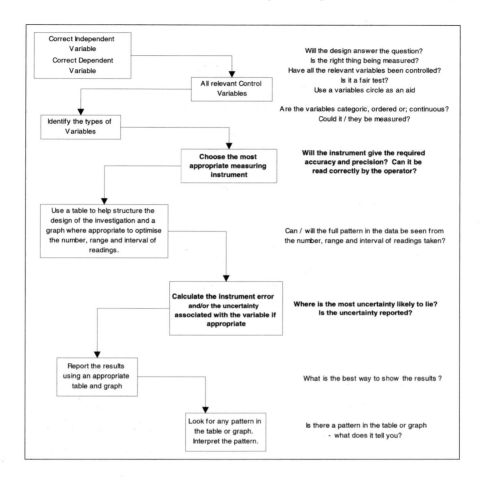

Correct Independent Variable
Correct Dependent Variable

Will the design answer the question?
Is the right thing being measured?
Have all the relevant variables been controlled?
Is it a fair test?
Use a variables circle as an aid

All relevant Control Variables

Are the variables categoric, ordered or; continuous?
Could it / they be measured?

Identify the types of Variables

Choose the most appropriate measuring instrument

Will the instrument give the required accuracy and precision? Can it be read correctly by the operator?

Use a table to help structure the design of the investigation and a graph where appropriate to optimise the number, range and interval of readings.

Can / will the full pattern in the data be seen from the number, range and interval of readings taken?

Calculate the instrument error and/or the uncertainty associated with the variable if appropriate

Where is the most uncertainty likely to lie? Is the uncertainty reported?

Report the results using an appropriate table and graph

What is the best way to show the results ?

Look for any pattern in the table or graph. Interpret the pattern.

Is there a pattern in the table or graph - what does it tell you?

Where are you?

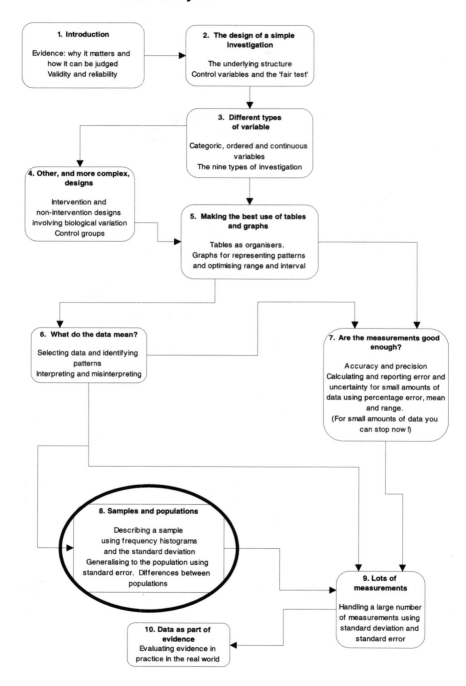

Chapter 8

Samples and populations

Introduction

> *Britain's tall teenagers want more designer clothes*

One of the examples used in the last chapter concerned the breaking strain of a wire. We looked at the problems associated with measurement errors and uncertainties of using a forcemeter. What we did not concern ourselves with was the wire itself. We, in general and not unreasonably, assume that one sample of wire will be so like another that we needn't worry about it. This is, of course, what the manufacturing industry and its quality control procedures are all about. So we pay for that consistency.

Sometimes, even small variations in the wire might be important. But the problem of such variation is more usually encountered in biological situations where one person, or plant, or animal cannot be said to be so like another. How do we handle that?

To begin with, we shall make an assumption in most of this chapter that there is no measurement error to worry about. This is clearly not always true, but it will simplify the argument. First we need some definitions:

A **population** is simply every possible member of the set. So if we are talking about the set of 'men', it is 'all men', if it is springer spaniels, it is 'all springer spaniels', and if it is wire, it is every bit of such wire.

A **sample** on the other hand, is whatever subset of that larger set (the population) that we either choose, or happen to have to hand. So we could have a sample of men which is the group who happen to work in the building, or springer spaniels in a breeding kennel, or wire from a particular manufacturer.

Let us take the springer spaniel example and assume we wanted to know their capacity to detect explosives via smell. Let us suppose, further, that we went to this breeder's kennels where we found 20 springers. When tested, there is bound to be a range of responses. There will be good sniffers, and poor ones. Ones that are easily distracted and the more determined. We can describe the sample; we can calculate the average for the group, and a range. The results for that group of spaniels are not open to doubt (assuming, as we said, no measurement error). But how representative of all spaniels are these measurements? Can we assume that spaniels in another area of the country will be equally good? Or were these an odd lot?

That is the question which provides the focus of this chapter – 'how can we describe the sample, and how can we make an estimate of how representative that sample is of the whole population?.

To begin with, we need to explore ways of describing the sample.

8.1 Describing the sample

Suppose you want to report the height of a sample of 16-year-old boys. You measure as many as you can. Of course, the boys will not all be the same height – you will find a range. But the more boys you measure, the more confident you will feel in the average, provided you choose randomly and do not pick all the small ones, or all the tall ones in the basketball team! Calculating the average is a starting point for describing the sample. The range also tells the reader the height of the tallest and shortest boys in the sample. But there are better ways of describing a sample which we describe below.

8.1.1 The frequency distribution

With lots of data it is a good idea to plot a 'frequency distribution'. A frequency distribution (which can be drawn by hand or, more easily, constructed with the help of a computer) gives you a visual picture of *all* the data. Compare this with the mean and the range which gives you three numbers and only *part* of the picture. What is a frequency distribution? A frequency distribution is just a graph of a 'tally' or count of the number of measurements. The count can be either of

- the number of measurements that are the same (as in the accuracy and precision of measurement histograms in the last chapter); or of

- the number of measurements in defined and consecutive groups/bands, as in the example that follows.

Suppose you were measuring the height of 16-year-old boys to the nearest centimetre. If you measured 10, then you might get these results:

Height (cm)
151
175
160
170
172
183
180
178
175
159

You could group these into bands – let us say 5 cm bands – counting how many measurements fall into each band like this:

Grouped heights (cm)	Frequency
151–155	1
156–160	2
161–165	0
166–170	1
171–175	3
176–180	2
181–185	1

From these grouped data, you can plot a frequency histogram:

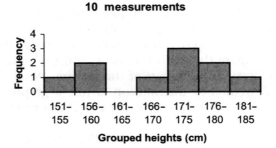

10 measurements

If you measured a total of fifty 16-year-old boys, the histogram might be more like this:

Grouped heights (cm)	Frequency
145-150	1
151-155	3
156-160	8
161-165	10
166-170	9
171-175	10
176-180	6
181-185	2
186-190	1

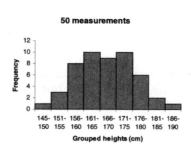

And 100 might look like this:

Grouped heights (cm)	Frequency
145-150	1
151-155	5
156-160	11
161-165	21
166-170	25
171-175	22
176-180	11
181-185	3
186-190	1

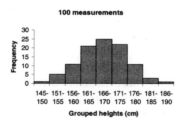

Notice how the histogram changes. Obviously with more readings, it gets taller (you need to imagine the scale on the y-axis staying the same). But you can also see that the shape of the histogram begins to settle down into a symmetrical shape as the number of measurements increases. If a vertical line was drawn down the middle, the two halves would be about the same size and mirror images of each other. This shape is known as a 'normal distribution'.[1] The data could be frequencies of almost anything, e.g. heights of students, pulse rates, heights of bounces of a ball, number of dandelions per square metre in pasture land, or the repeated readings of a measuring instrument. Many naturally occurring phenomena behave like this, which is why many statistical treatments are based on it – it is very widely applicable.

Think about the mean height for 16-year-old boys. Where would you expect the mean to be on the frequency distribution?

☆ ☆ ☆ ☆ ☆ ☆

1 There are occasions when the distribution will be skewed. For example, if you were plotting frequencies of students' marks in a very difficult examination – the bell-shape would be 'skewed' towards the left hand side or the lower marks: it would not be symmetrical.

The mean will lie in the middle of the normal distribution. The readings at the extreme sides are the infrequent very high or very low measurements. In this case, these are the particularly short or the unusually tall 16-year-old boys.

☆ ☆ ☆ ☆ ☆ ☆

If you took a lot more readings, you could then easily draw a line through the top of the bars of the histogram to define a bell-shaped curve. The bell can be tall and thin or short and fat depending on the choice of scale of the graph but *its proportions will always be the same for a particular set of data*. The more readings you take, the smoother the curve:

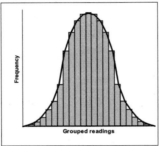

Once you have plotted a frequency distribution of your data, you will have a feel for its shape. You might then calculate the mean and identify the range. Why are the mean and range alone not enough? Consider the following.

Suppose we're looking at the alcohol intake of two neighbourhoods (A and B) who are reported to have alcohol-related problems. The alcohol consumption of both neighbourhoods is, on average, the same: 10 units per day. When the data are grouped and plotted on a frequency histogram, they look like this.

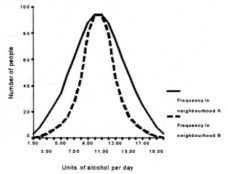

The distributions show that although the means are the same, the spread of the data is very different. Suppose 15 units per day is viewed as problematic by the local council in terms of anti-social behaviour. Then looking at the means (10 units per day), neither of the areas has a problem. The range would tell us that that there are some heavy and some light drinkers in both Neighbourhoods. But the distribution shows that Neighbourhood A has a much greater alcohol problem: many more people drink more than 10 units per day than in Neighbourhood B.

But supposing the distribution was like this:

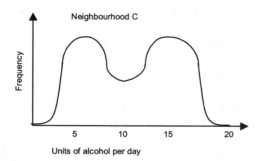

This sort of distribution, which is clearly not the bell-shaped normal distribution, suggests that there are two different groups in Neighbourhood C, one with a mean at 5 units per day and one with a mean at 15 units per day (women and men?). Note that the simple statistics that follow are based on the 'normal' distribution so that if the distribution of the frequencies of the data has another shape, for example, like Neighbourhood C, you will need to consult a statistics text to consider how the data may be reported.

☆ ☆ ☆ ☆ ☆ ☆

If the shape of your data suggests a normal distribution, then you can calculate a statistic called the 'standard deviation'.

8.1.2 The standard deviation (SD)

The standard deviation[2] is a much better and stronger depiction of the shape of the data than the mean and the range and is used and quoted

---

[2] The mathematical formula for the standard deviation is as follows (most calculators or spreadsheets will work this figure out for you):

$$s = \sqrt{\frac{\sum (x - \bar{x})^2}{n}}$$

where s = standard deviation of the sample
x = a single measurement
$\bar{x}$ = mean
n = number of measurements/sample size

widely. Although the frequency distribution gives you a good visual picture of the data, the standard deviation is a way of summarising the shape of the distribution as a quantity, as a single figure. It is a way of reporting the spread of the data around the mean *of the actual measurements you have taken.* In this way, it is similar to the range but the SD is different because it also reports the 'average' amount by which the measurements deviate from the mean and so tells you the shape of the bell in the normal distribution. Like the range:

- the greater the spread of the measurements, the greater the standard deviation;
- the smaller the spread, the smaller the standard deviation.

But, unlike the range:

- Very low or very high values – rogues, outliers – have less of an influence on the description of the spread.

The symmetrical shape of the distribution means that we can work out what proportion of the measurements lie between any two values of the variable. The simplest example is to take the mean and the maximum (or the mean and the minimum). You can see that half the measurements (or 50 per cent) would lie either side of the midline.

One standard deviation is also a fixed proportion of the measurements. The mean plus or minus one standard deviation (see next diagram) is the area in the 'middle' of the bell before the sides begin to 'bend out' (at points of 'inflection'). It includes about two-thirds (68 per cent) of the measurements. There is no magic to the figure but we have to choose something!

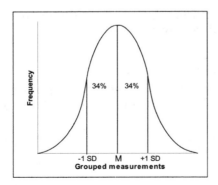
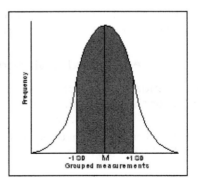

So, if we were to take another reading at random, then it would probably fall within one standard deviation either side of the mean (the shaded area in the above right hand figure). It is likely that two out of three readings would fall within this range.

We can extend the range to two standard deviations which represents 95 per cent of the area under the normal curve:

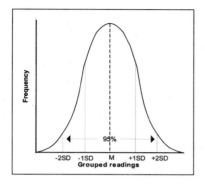 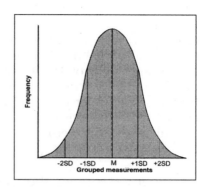

If we took another reading now, it would almost certainly lie within the range plus or minus two standard deviations from the mean (the shaded area in the above right-hand figure). It is likely that 19 out of 20 readings (or 95 out of 100 readings) would fall within these limits.

To recap, the standard deviation is a more useful number than the range because[3]:

- it describes the way the actual data are spread around the mean;
- it quantifies the shape of the data;
- it enables prediction of the likelihood (or probability) of subsequent measurements of the same variable.

8.1.3 Examples of using standard deviation to describe lots of data

The standard deviation is particularly useful in 'looking back' at measurements. The SD gives you a feel for the shape of the data without actually 'seeing' every measurement.

As a simple example, suppose the mean examination score for a physics exam this year is 60 marks and the standard deviation 15 marks (60 ± 15). This tells you that 68 per cent of the students scored marks of between 45 and 75 (60–15 ↔ 60 + 15). It also tells you that only 5 per cent of students scored marks of less than 30 or more than 90 (± 2SDs).

☆ ☆ ☆ ☆ ☆ ☆

---

[3] These characteristics of the standard deviation apply provided the sample is random. We shall make this assumption from here on.

Try these:

1. You read that two laboratories have used different methods to measure levels of a substance in the blood. Laboratory 1's results are 281.6 ± 6.1 while Laboratory 2's results are 279.9 ± 3.1. Sketch the shape of the data by sketching both on one frequency distribution. Assuming that they have both carried out the same number of repeated readings, which laboratory's results are more reliable (assuming normal distributions)?
2. The mean height of 16-year-old boys is 170 cm and the standard deviation is ± 10 cm. If the minimum height for a theme park ride is 160 cm, what percentage of boys would you expect to be refused entry by the supervisor (assuming a normal distribution and that the rules were followed)?

8.1.4 What determines the spread in measurements, and therefore the standard deviation, of the sample?

The basic shape of the normal distribution is determined by:

- the spread due to the 'natural' variation of the sample itself;
- any error and uncertainty in the measurements. The more uncertain the measurements, the wider the spread (or the distribution).

The number in the sample (or the sample size) only influences the shape by random variation. So, as the sample increases in size, the shape eventually 'settles' down to the normal distribution. Beyond this point, increasing the number of measurements will not change the standard deviation.

8.1.5 Using standard deviation to predict: probability and risk

You will already have noticed that the bell shape of the normal distribution enables us to predict where the next measurement is likely to be. This means that we can estimate the risk or the probability of future measurements lying within the limits specified by the standard deviation.

Taking our example of the heights of boys again, a clothing manufacturer can use the information to determine the most popular sizes of clothes. They will know that the chances of boys being between certain heights around the average height (165 cm) is great. So they can make lots of clothes of these sizes. For boys who are especially tall, they will know how many of them there are likely to be and decide whether or not to produce clothes for this small group. Of course, for adults, most large scale manufacturers decide that it is not worthwhile making clothes to suit the very tall – the top end of the normal distribution. Hence, the advent of outsize shops!

At the individual level, if you know the mean and standard deviation (165 and 10 say), then you can predict the height of the next boy to come into the room and assign odds to your prediction. For instance, there is only a 1 in 40 chance that the next boy to come through the door will be more than two SDs taller than the average – that is more than 185 cm tall.

8.1.6 The effect of changing the population definition

Instead of measuring any 16-year-old boys, we might limit our measurements to boys in the UK. We might also exclude those boys born and brought up outside the UK since their diet might have been different during critical growth periods. Clearly we are restricting the population from which the sample is to be drawn, which is likely to have the effect of decreasing the range and standard deviation.

☆ ☆ ☆ ☆ ☆ ☆

To make sure you understand what standard deviation means, try the following:

1 Gazelles

The number of gazelles in a National Park in Kenya is recorded monthly at the beginning of the month. The national park has one open boundary so that the gazelles can move in and out of the park freely. The total number therefore fluctuates. Here are the figures for five years with standard deviations:

Year	Mean weekly population ±SD
1969	373 ± 68
1970	363 ± 47
1971	405 ± 63
1972	408 ± 57
1973	388 ± 56

- In 1971 the mean was 405 and the SD 63. What does that tell you about the number of gazelles in the area week by week?
- In which year was the number of gazelles in the area at its most stable?
- In 1971, for about how many weeks was the number less than 342 (the mean –1 SD)?

8.2 Summary so far

Collecting a lot of data means we can get a better picture of the variation or uncertainty in a sample of data. The normal frequency
distribution and the standard deviation serve to report the variation.
Both can also be used to predict subsequent measurements.

The standard deviation is a better way of reporting data than the
range because it gives the reader a feel for the shape of the data and
reports where most of the measurements lie. As a rule of thumb, it is
not sensible to calculate standard deviations for less than 20 measurements; ideally, it should be used for a lot of data. But you will often
find it used for very much smaller numbers. Then you need to watch
out for what is done with the data, and treat any generalisations with
a degree of scepticism. It is good practice to include the total sample
size in any report.

8.3 The limitations of the standard deviation

The trouble with the standard deviation is that it only describes the
distribution of the sample of measurements that you have collected.
Let us take the example we used before of the height of 16-year-old
boys. We ended up with 100 measurements and a frequency distribution which was approaching the shape of a normal distribution. So we
could have calculated the standard deviation.

Supposing we now take another sample of 100 16-year-old boys.
Would we get exactly the same distribution? Probably not. We might
get something like Sample 2 in the following frequency distribution:

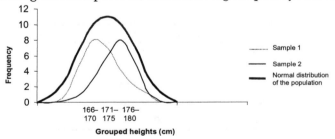

You can see that the mean of Sample 2 is slightly different and that
these 100 boys tend to be a bit taller. What is the 'true' mean height
of 16-year-old boys?

What we need to do is somehow describe not just the sample, but the
whole 'population'. Population here refers to all values of the variable in
question – in this case the height of *all* 16-year-old boys. It would be
impossible to measure all 16-year-old boys but fortunately we have a statistic which enables us to calculate what the true mean value might be.

Much of (inferential) statistics aims to define the relationship between the sample of measurements we can take in reality and this ideal distribution of *all* possible measurements – which is often a very large number.

8.4 Describing the population:

8.4.1 The standard deviation of the means or the standard error (SE)

Suppose you could continue to take random samples from a population and for each sample you calculated the mean. There will be some variation in that mean since, by chance, there are likely to be more tall boys in one sample than in another for instance.

Sample	Number of boys in sample	Mean height (cm)
1	100	163
2	100	157
3	100	161
Etc.		

Then you could draw a frequency distribution of the counts of the *means* in the same way as you did a frequency distribution of the measurements (see page 142). What would a frequency histogram *of all possible sample means* look like? As you may have guessed, it would approximate to the bell-shaped normal distribution. The sample means will cluster around the true mean of the population. In other words, the sample means will themselves have a mean. (Keep going!) Notice the change in the x-axis label.

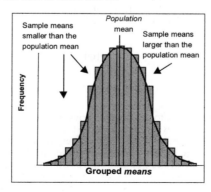

Notice, too, that the sample means that are smaller than the 'true' population mean will lie to the left of the vertical midline in the bell and sample means that are larger will lie to the right hand side.

In reality, of course, you rarely if ever, see a distribution like this. Usually we have only or two samples. From our knowledge of the normal distribution, we know that the shape means we can estimate the standard deviation of the means. But this time it is not the standard deviation of the raw frequencies – it is the *standard deviation of the means*. This is the standard error (SE).[4]

8.4.2 Confidence limits

Since 68 per cent of the sample means lie in the body of the bell, it is likely that our sample mean will be within one SE of the mean.

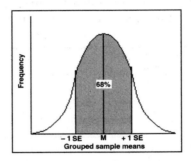

4 Let us take a look at the formula for SE. It is simply the standard deviation of the sample divided by the square root of the number of readings (n).

$$SE = \frac{s}{\sqrt{n}}$$

Suppose in our example the mean of 100 random measurements is 169 and the standard deviation is 6. What is the 'true' mean for all boys in the country likely to be?
The standard error is calculated as follows:

$$SE = \frac{6}{\sqrt{100}}$$

$$SE = \frac{6}{10} = 0.6$$

So our best guess at the mean for all possible boys is 169 ± 0.6. We are saying that it is 68 per cent likely, or two chances in three, that the true mean lies between 168.4 and 169.6. It is 95 per cent likely, 19 in 20, that it lies between 167.8 and 170.2 (within 2 SE).
(We have omitted a stage in this calculation related to the difference between the SD of the sample and the SD of the population. For our purposes here, where we are making an estimate of the uncertainty, we shall not go into this distinction but refer the interested reader to a statistics book [e.g. Pentz, M. and Shott, M. (1988) *Handling Experimental Data*, Open University Press].)

These are known as the 68 per cent 'confidence limits'. This means that any single reading we take is 68 per cent (about two-thirds) likely to be within plus or minus one standard error in the 'true' mean. So we have defined the confidence we can place in the sample mean. We have used the statistic to quantify the uncertainty about the sample in relation to the population from which the sample is drawn. The area representing plus or minus two standard errors is known as the 95 per cent 'confidence limits'. So any new sample mean is 95 per cent likely to lie within this wider range.

You can see that the SE is a powerful statistic because it gives us estimates about the whole population rather than just describing the sample of measurements we have taken. It enables us to *generalise* about the population as a whole *from one sample*. It is important to realise that we can never know the real or 'true' population mean unless we measure every member of that population – in other words when the sample is equal to the population. At this point, clearly, there can be no sampling error.

8.4.3 What affects the standard error?

The smaller the SE, the closer any sample mean is likely to be to the true mean of the population. So we are aiming for as small a SE as possible. How can we reduce the SE?

It seems sensible that if you increase the size of the sample, you are going to have a better picture of the population and you will be more confident about your generalisation. But you will have to take a lot more readings to make it smaller.[5]

Knowing that the SE is the standard deviation of the distribution of the sample means, then it follows that if the spread or dispersion of the sample means is decreased, then the deviation of the SE will decrease. One way in which the standard deviation can be decreased would be by increasing the accuracy of our measurements of height. But often,

---

[5] So in our example of 100 boys' heights, if we increase the sample by a factor of 100 to 10,000, then the standard error will reduce by the square root of 10,000 or 100 to 0.06.

$$SE = 6/\sqrt{10,000}$$

$$SE = 6/100$$

$$= 0.06$$

So increasing the sample by a factor of x100 has reduced the SE only by a factor of 10.

the range in boys' heights will be far greater than any uncertainty in the measuring of any one height. There is nothing you can then do to reduce the spread in the readings – that is what boys are like!

8.4.4 Choosing a sample size

How do we know what size of sample is big enough to give a meaningful description of the population? If we take too small a sample, it is unlikely to be representative. If we take too large a sample, it would waste time and money unnecessarily. The size of the sample depends to some extent on the purpose of the exercise although as a general rule, the more confident we can be in the data the better.

It is often worth doing a pilot study to estimate the likely standard error. If the standard deviation seems large, then you will need a bigger sample than if it is low. If the cost of making incorrect generalisations about the population is high (we might be talking about the risk of fatal side effects of a drug for instance), then we should aim for 95 per cent or even 99 per cent confidence limits. But this may have to be weighed against the cost of collecting data from a very large sample.

8.5 Differences between populations

The statistics described above are particularly useful when we want to establish whether there is a significant difference between two (or more) values of a variable.

Let us take some real examples so that we can see why 'a difference' might matter:

- A market gardener suspects that there is no difference in the yield of tomatoes from two varieties of tomato seeds, one of which is considerably cheaper.
- A pharmaceutical company wants to find out whether drug A produced by a competitor is more effective than their own or 'in-house' drug B in reducing levels of blood sugar in diabetic patients.

In each of these examples we have two variables (the variety of tomato seed is the independent variable and tomato yield is the dependent variable; drug type and level of blood sugar are the equivalent in example 2). The question is whether there is a significant difference between the two values of the independent variable. Let us look closer at the tomato seed example.

8.5.1 The problem

Suppose the market gardener plants the two varieties of seed, variety A and variety B. So:

- the *sample* is the number of seeds of each variety planted (we will limit it to 5 here for clarity in the diagrams below);
- the *population* is all the seeds of that variety (an unknown number in reality).

The market gardener measures the yield per plant. We might find that the two sets of measurements (represented here by the black and white circles) look very different in that they are quite far apart and so obviously different.

In that case, the answer is straightforward. But we might find that the yields are more like this, with larger ranges and a degree of overlap:

Here is another way of considering this:

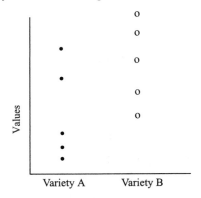

Is Variety A better than Variety B? How do we know whether or not they are from the same population or whether they are from two different populations (i.e. is there a significant difference between the two Varieties)?

Let us increase the number of plants to 10 from each variety (it should be a lot more than 10 of course before we could use this sort of statistics sensibly, but let's keep it simple for now). First we measure the yield of ripe tomatoes produced by each plant.

	Variety A	Variety B
Plant 1	2.8	2.9
Plant 2	2.5	2.6
Plant 3	2.8	2.9
Plant 4	3.0	3.1
Plant 5	2.9	3.0
Plant 6	2.7	2.8
Plant 7	2.7	2.7
Plant 8	2.6	2.6
Plant 9	2.6	2.6
Plant 10	2.8	2.8
Mean	2.74	2.80
Standard error	0.05	0.06

The standard errors show an overlap between Variety A and Variety B:

Mean ± 1SE = Variety A 2.74 ± 0.05 or 2.69 ↔ 2.79
= Variety B 2.8 ± 0.06 or 2.74 ↔ 2.86

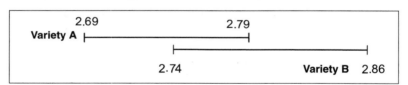

If we plotted these measurements as a frequency distribution, the frequencies would also overlap like this:

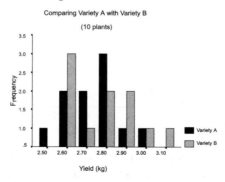

The first thing to remind ourselves of is that, *for this sample,* Variety B produces a better yield. But that is not what we want to know. We want to know whether the *variety* as a whole is better. It could be that another sample of 10 plants would make Variety A better. We can't be sure that the two types of tomato seed are really different. We need to estimate the population means – in other words what does the sample allow us to say about what the yield would be like if we had every possible tomato plant of these two varieties in our greenhouse?

If we plot the means and standard errors of the samples of Variety A and Variety B, the bar chart looks like the one that follows. Note that the lighter areas represent ± 1SE.[6]

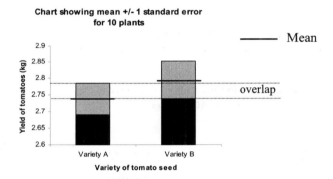

Again, you can see the overlap clearly; you cannot see daylight between the two bar charts – you cannot say that the *populations* (all the members of the two Varieties) are really different. This answer could have arisen by chance. What we are aiming to do is to try to see if we can reduce the standard error so that there is no overlap so that we can be reasonably confident (68 per cent) that the two Varieties are different.

We know that one way of decreasing the standard error is to increase the number of measurements substantially. So we could take some more measurements to increase the number to 100 measurements.

The figures then might be:

Mean ± SE = Variety A 2.74 ± 0.02 or 2.72 ↔ 2.76
= Variety B 2.8 ± 0.02 or 2.8 ↔ 2.82

Our frequency distribution now looks like this:

---

6 In statistics textbooks, you will find this idea presented differently in terms of the standard error of differences between the means.

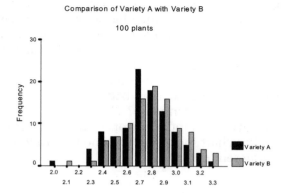

The distributions of the two groups are becoming a little clearer to separate out. The associated bar chart confirms this:

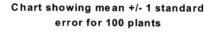

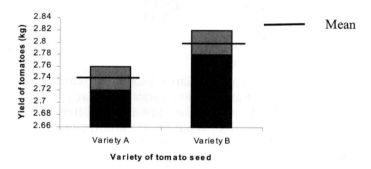

There is no overlap between the two areas that are shaded grey. One standard error allows us to be 68 per cent confident that the two varieties of tomato seeds produce different yields of tomatoes. Variety B produces a greater yield.

But notice that if we want to be 95 per cent confident (± 2 SEs), the following bar chart shows that there is still some overlap – so we cannot be that certain:

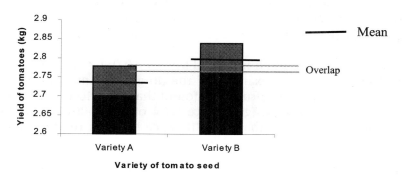

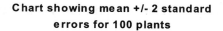

If we want to try to be 95% confident, we could try growing more plants and take more measurements.

So how big a sample is needed?

Again, as we saw in the last chapter, it is a matter of judgement. The market gardener could decide, for instance, that if the difference between the two varieties were less than 10 per cent, then he wouldn't really care which type he planted. The sample we are looking for, then, is one that would give standard errors which allow us to be 68 per cent (for instance) sure that there is a 10 per cent difference in the yields. So you increase the sample until that point is reached by trial and error and educated guesswork.

8.5.2 More complex statistics

Standard errors are the basis of more complex statistics for testing whether the difference between two values of a variable (or varieties of tomato) is significant. The statistical approach is to start from the assumption that they are from the same population (the 'null hypothesis') unless the data prove otherwise. For details of particular statistical tests of difference, the reader is encouraged to turn to an appropriate statistical text. Suffice it to say here that most computers can perform these tests very easily.

The output of these kinds of statistics are reported in terms of the probability of the difference between two sets of measurements occurring by chance. So, if $p < 0.05$ then this means that the probability of the difference occurring by chance is less than 5 per cent (or less than 1 in 20). The three probability levels most commonly reported are:

- $p < 0.05$ (less than 5 per cent or less than 1 in 20).
- $p < 0.01$ (less than 1 per cent or less than 1 in 100)
- $p < 0.001$ (less than 0.1 per cent or less than 1 in 1000).

These levels are also often indicated by * ($p < 0.05$), ** ($p < 0.01$) or *** ($p < 0.001$). So in our example, if the drug company compared the effectiveness of the two drugs and found that the effect of drug A differed from drug B at a significance level of $p < 0.001$, it would be reasonable to conclude that the difference between the two drugs is significant.

8.6 Is there a change?

In the last section, we considered whether there was a significant *difference* between two populations. But we might be more interested in whether there was a *change* in two sets of measurements from the *same population* but taken at two (or more) different times.[7] To see if there is a significant change, we can use similar statistics to those already described. The only difference is that the measurements can be matched because they are the same individuals. This tends to reduce variation and allow us to use more powerful statistics.

We can compare 'difference' and 'change' as follows:

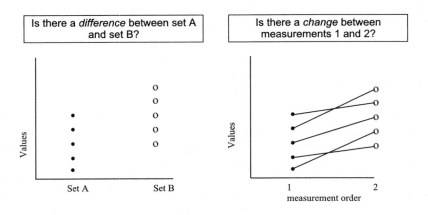

---

[7] There is a statistical assumption here, namely that the changes will be normally distributed.

In the first case, we are looking at the *difference* between two quite separate populations and so the statistics concerns the means of the two populations. In the second case, we are interested in the *change* between the same individuals on two occasions. So the statistics focuses on the difference between each pair of readings.

Why might a change be important? Here are some examples:

- Does the vitamin content of a type of apple change between the time of picking and the sell-by date?
- Does the level of hormone X in patients differ significantly before and after treatment with a drug?
- Does the composition of unstable chemicals change when tested on subsequent days?

In looking at change, we are interested in the matched *pairs* of readings: so, in the second example, we can compare the level of hormone X in the same patient after administration of the drug. We can *pair* the readings for each patient and then consider whether the change in the population as a whole is significant. The question becomes 'do most patients show a significant change?'

8.7 Summary

In this chapter we have considered ways of describing a sample using:

- the standard deviation;
- the standard error.

The standard error is a means of generalising from the sample to the population.

We have also considered the use of these statistics in determining probability, choosing a sample size and in finding out whether or not there is a difference between two populations. The same statistics can be used to examine the change between two or more variables.

8.8 Looking forward, looking back

In looking forward we need to decide how big a sample to take to give reliable readings which will enable us to generalise from the results

and look for a difference or change. In looking back, we can consider
how any statistics presented enable us to decide how much confidence
can be placed in the data. Quantifying uncertainty in this way enables
us to judge the reliability of the data as a part of evidence.

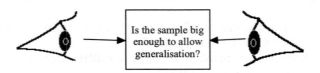

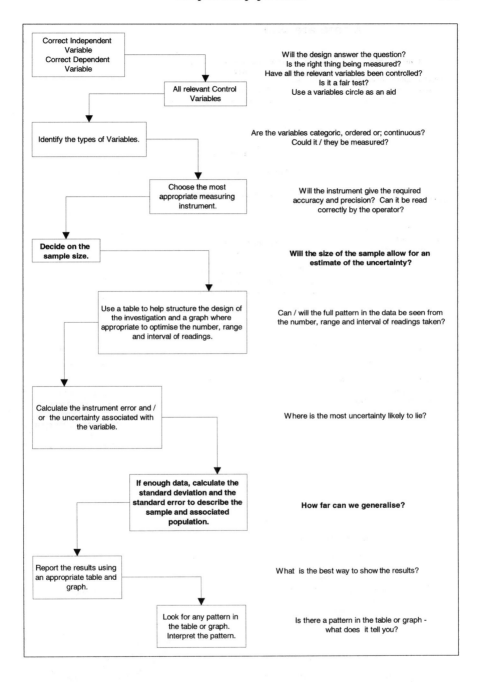

Correct Independent Variable
Correct Dependent Variable

Will the design answer the question?
Is the right thing being measured?
Have all the relevant variables been controlled?
Is it a fair test?
Use a variables circle as an aid

All relevant Control Variables

Identify the types of Variables.

Are the variables categoric, ordered or; continuous?
Could it / they be measured?

Choose the most appropriate measuring instrument.

Will the instrument give the required accuracy and precision? Can it be read correctly by the operator?

Decide on the sample size.

Will the size of the sample allow for an estimate of the uncertainty?

Use a table to help structure the design of the investigation and a graph where appropriate to optimise the number, range and interval of readings.

Can / will the full pattern in the data be seen from the number, range and interval of readings taken?

Calculate the instrument error and / or the uncertainty associated with the variable.

Where is the most uncertainty likely to lie?

If enough data, calculate the standard deviation and the standard error to describe the sample and associated population.

How far can we generalise?

Report the results using an appropriate table and graph.

What is the best way to show the results?

Look for any pattern in the table or graph. Interpret the pattern.

Is there a pattern in the table or graph - what does it tell you?

Where are you?

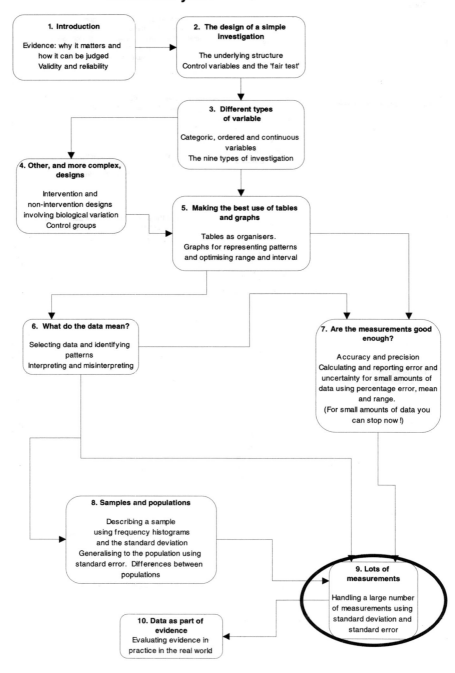

1. Introduction

Evidence: why it matters and how it can be judged
Validity and reliability

2. The design of a simple investigation

The underlying structure
Control variables and the 'fair test'

3. Different types of variable

Categoric, ordered and continuous variables
The nine types of investigation

4. Other, and more complex, designs

Intervention and non-intervention designs involving biological variation
Control groups

5. Making the best use of tables and graphs

Tables as organisers.
Graphs for representing patterns and optimising range and interval

6. What do the data mean?

Selecting data and identifying patterns
Interpreting and misinterpreting

7. Are the measurements good enough?

Accuracy and precision
Calculating and reporting error and uncertainty for small amounts of data using percentage error, mean and range.
(For small amounts of data you can stop now !)

8. Samples and populations

Describing a sample using frequency histograms and the standard deviation
Generalising to the population using standard error. Differences between populations

9. Lots of measurements

Handling a large number of measurements using standard deviation and standard error

10. Data as part of evidence
Evaluating evidence in practice in the real world

Chapter 9

Lots of measurements

Introduction

What are the chances of the bungee jumper hitting the water?

In this chapter, we will consider how the simple statistics we introduced in the previous chapter in describing samples and populations can be used in the same way when handling lots of repeated measurements. In chapter 8, we looked at the problems associated with predicting from a sample to the population. In most cases the population is defined – it might be impossible to use all the population, or even to quantify it. The population of 'all springer spaniels' for instance is finite but very difficult to pin down, but, in theory we could gather up all the springer spaniels in the world and measure something about the population.

In this chapter we are going to look at the issues that arise when you try to predict from a sample to an undefined population – of measurements of a variable. The number of such measurements is, in principle, infinite – but, other than that, the statistics work in exactly the same way.

In Chapter 7 we saw that, by careful inspection of the measuring instruments and procedures in an experiment or investigation, we can estimate where the most uncertainty in making measurements is likely to be. We also saw that:

- A single measurement is unlikely to be reliable as a measure of the 'true' value;
- A few repeated measurements can give us an indication as to whether our estimate of the size of the uncertainty is sensible.

A large number of measurements will, as we shall see in what follows, give us more confidence that we know how uncertain our measurement really is and can enable us to predict probability and risk.

9.1 Why is taking a lot of measurements a 'good thing'

This might seem an obvious question but it will be useful to clarify our thinking here as to why a few measurements are not enough.

Take the example of a typical school science experiment in which a chemical or powder (or indigestion/hangover pills) is added to a liquid and as a result of the chemical reaction which takes place, a gas (usually carbon dioxide) is given off. The pupils are asked to record the time taken for 20cm^3 of gas to be emitted. Each group does the experiment three times and the results vary a bit both within each group and between different groups. Why do the results vary?

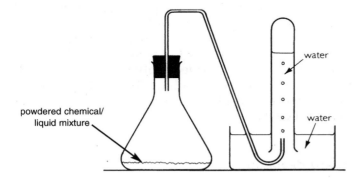

The variation could be due to:

- errors in making the measurements.

For example, the equipment for collecting gas is always tricky – there can easily be a few leaks in the system. Timing this experiment is also awkward – you have to be very quick to start and stop the timer (human error).

- uncertainty in the variable to be measured due to uncontrolled variables.

The mass of the powder, or the temperature of the liquid might be slightly different. Stirring may vary from one measurement to another. There are always variables that you can never quite keep the same, or which are simply too expensive to control effectively.

What you can do, however, is to repeat the measurement often enough so that you know the extent of these errors and uncertainties – all of them contribute to the distribution of a set of readings, to the range and standard deviation. With enough readings you can estimate the 'true' value.

9.2 Describing a lot of measurements

Just as in the previous chapter we began by considering the sample, and how it can be described and used, we shall do the same here. The sample is now, however, how many repeated readings of the same measurement we decide to take.

9.2.1 The average and the range

Working out the average (mean) of all the repeated measurements is the obvious starting point. That, together with the range, gives you some idea of the 'shape' of the distribution of measurements. But the mean can, as we have seen, represent a set of readings which are very close together, or a set where there is wide variation. The range can be exaggerated with one 'outlier'; a rogue reading. To get a better feel for the distribution of the repeated readings we turn, as we did in the last chapter, to the standard deviation.

9.2.2 The standard deviation

Just as in sampling tomato plants, we can envisage the repeated measurements you have taken as a sample. Standard deviation is a way of describing the distribution of these repeated measurements about the mean and of quantifying the shape of the frequency distribution. It also enables prediction of the likelihood of the value of the next measurement.

9.2.3 Using standard deviation to predict: probability and risk

Remember that the bell shape of the normal distribution enables us both to describe the readings we have and to predict where the next measurement is likely to be. This means that we can estimate the risk or the probability of future measurements lying within chosen limits.

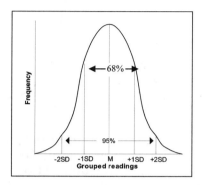

Let us think ourselves into the position of a bungee rope manufacturer. The ideal rope will be:

- very stretchy to give lots of bounce;
- reliably strong – broken ropes are not good for business;
- predictable – you need to know how far bungee jumpers will fall;
- exciting – the closer to the ground/water the person falls, the more exciting the experience.

When you jump, there will always be slight variations in how you jump, how streamlined you manage to look on the way down (wildly flailing arms will slow you down!) and so on. This will result in slight differences in how far the bungee jumper will fall. Sometimes they will fall rather further because they were going faster. Other times they will be slightly slower.

Supposing you test the same rope 100 times. You record the distance fallen by a dummy bungee jumper (we shall assume that the operator has decided to set some maximum weight for the jumpers and is going to test the rope at that weight!). There will be variation in the measured value of drop height due to errors and uncertainties in the measurement process itself, as well as uncontrolled variation in the conditions for each fall – wind, slightly different attitude of the dummy jumper, and so on. Let us suppose, for ease, that the average fall is 100 feet. But it is not the average that is the most important figure here. You calculate the standard deviation as ±5 feet. Suppose one of your customers is an operator who wants to set his crane (the jumping off point) at 100 feet.

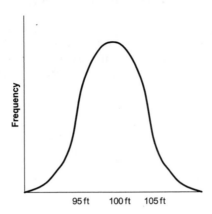

Fifty percent of his customers would hit the ground/water because the rope is likely to stretch to more than 100 feet for half of the jumps. To put it another way, if you jumped from his crane you would have a 50 per cent chance, or risk, or probability of being badly injured. But the most likely thing to happen is that you would *just* hit the ground.

Suppose the crane is raised to 105 feet. This is the value of the mean plus one standard deviation. Knowing that 68 per cent of the measurements fall within 1SD, means that 32 per cent fall outside this range. So the probability of a jump being lower or higher than 95–105 feet is 32 per cent (or 32 in 100). We can reduce this risk to 16 per cent because we are only interested in the rope stretching further than 105 feet. It doesn't matter if it extends to less than 95 feet. So now we can predict that about 16 in 100 people will hit the ground/water. Or that your chance, as the next jumper, will be about one in six of coming to a sticky end. Still not very good for the business.

☆ ☆ ☆ ☆ ☆ ☆

1. What would the risk of hitting the ground/water be if the crane was raised to 110 feet?
2. Similarly in our indigestion powder example, supposing the students tell you that the reaction time (as measured by the time for 20cm^3 of gas to be emitted) is 130 ± 5 sec (mean ± 1SD). Ninety-five per cent of all repeated measurements will be within what range?

☆ ☆ ☆ ☆ ☆ ☆

9.2.4 Reducing variation

The narrower the frequency distribution, and therefore the smaller the standard deviation, the more confidence we would have in our predictions as to whether disaster looms. Can we reduce the variation in the measurements? The frequency distribution will then be narrower and the standard deviation will be smaller. The aim always is to try to *reduce* the variation. How can this be done?

One way of decreasing the variation is to improve the measurement method. For example, in the case of the bungee rope, it could be that the measurement of drop height was made against a tall 'ruler' graduated in 6 inch intervals perhaps. So the person trying to measure the lowest point will be hampered by:

- the fact that the 'person' on the end of the rope is moving, so it is difficult to measure the lowest point of the fall;
- the additional problem that the instrument is only marked every 6 inch making reading distances in between the 6 inch marks difficult – instrument error.

If the person doing the recording were replaced by a high speed video camera and a scale graduated in 3 inch intervals, then the spread in the measurements due to error will be less, and so will the standard deviation of the ensuing data. If the standard deviation can be reduced, through more accurate measurement, to 2 feet rather than 5 feet, then we would be able to predict the chances of disaster with a little more confidence.

Although we can aim to minimise error and increase accuracy of measurement, it is difficult to reduce uncertainty. For instance, it is unrealistic to control every possible variable that might affect the measurement. So there is a limit to how far the standard deviation can be reduced. There is also the reality of the situation – you cannot expect a bungee jumper to follow precise instructions!

Before you read on, try the following:

Squash balls
A manufacturer needs to find out which is the best way to measure the rebound height of the squash balls he produces. He wants a reliable method but he does not want to spend money unnecessarily on expensive equipment (but let us not worry about the expense at this stage). So he asks for tests to be run on three measurement

methods (50 repeated measurements of each method). Here are the results:

	Mean rebound height (cm)	Standard deviation
By eye	37.58	2.73
Using a video to record the rebound height	38.01	2.71
Sophisticated electronic equipment	37.17	1.70

- Comment on the three methods.
- What would you suggest to the manufacturer? (He will also, of course, have to consider cost.)

In a primary school, a teacher had two consecutive science classes doing this simple investigation:

> Find out how the dissolving time of sugar is related to the size of the sugar grains.

Towards the end of the first practical, the class pooled their results, each group writing their results on the blackboard. The teacher noticed that some of the children were stirring the sugar/water solution while others were not. She decided to tell the next class to stir the mixture steadily until the sugar dissolved. The following are sketches of the shapes of the resulting frequency histograms for the dissolving time of the same type of sugar.

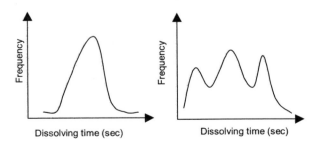

Which is the frequency histogram from the class where stirring was *not* well-controlled?

9.2.5 Standard error

Just as we saw in the last chapter, the standard deviation is limited to describing the measurements you have taken. The sample of repeated measurements could, by chance, have all been a little low, or high, or bunched closely together. The standard error (or the standard deviation of the means) is a way of generalising to all possible repeated measurements and estimating where the 'true' mean is.

Let us take the example we used before of bungee jumping. We ended up with 100 measurements of the distance fallen by a dummy bungee jumper. Supposing we now take another sample of 100 measurements. Would we get exactly the same distribution and the same mean? Probably not. We might get something like this:

Sample	Number of jumps	Mean drop height (metres)
1	100	98
2	100	101
3	100	102
etc		

You could then draw a frequency distribution of these means and, preferably with a lot more samples, calculate the standard errors and confidence limits in the same way as we did in the last chapter.

The standard error so calculated is now the best estimate we can have for the 'error bars' which tell us the likelihood that the true value lies within them. In our bungee example at the beginning of this chapter (page 167), for instance, we measured an average drop height (the sample mean) of 100ft with a standard deviation of 5ft. The standard error can be calculated from this in the same way as in the last chapter and gives us:

$$Standard\ error = \frac{Standard\ deviation}{\sqrt{Number\ of\ readings}}$$

$$= \frac{5}{\sqrt{100}}$$

$$= 0.5$$

So our best guess is that the true mean of the drop height is 68 per cent likely to be between 99.5 and 100.5 feet.

What affects the standard error?
From the above formula, it is clear that the standard error is affected by the size of

- the standard deviation and
- the number of readings.

We know (see section 9.2.4) that the standard deviation can be decreased by improving the measurement method and, of course, by reducing any other error (e.g. minimising human error). But a degree of uncertainty (due to all the uncontrolled variables) will always remain. Increasing the number of readings will decrease the standard error but, because the formula uses the square root of the number of readings, then you will need to do a lot more readings for a small reduction in the standard error.

Again there is an element of judgement depending on the purpose of the measurement. The decision as to whether it is worthwhile buying more sophisticated measuring instruments or spending time on taking a lot more readings will depend on how critical the measurements are.

9.3 What about errors and uncertainties?

In chapter 7, taking a few measurements, we discussed the problem of estimating errors and uncertainties in each measurement, combining them and making a judgement as to which was the most significant. We also noted that systematic error is particularly problematic since it is only by reference to independent measurements or a standard that it is likely to be exposed. The spread of a large number of measurements takes into account all sources of error and uncertainty *except* systematic error – that's why we must always be aware of the dangers of systematic error!

When you have a large number of readings, it is reasonably safe to say that all possible sources of error are contained within the range of measurements. That range will be caused by human error, instrument error, uncertainty due to uncontrolled variables and so on. You won't know which is the most significant just by looking at the data, but you will know the results are likely to be representative. So the only reason you would need to estimate the errors due to a particular measuring instrument for instance, would be to work out whether those errors were large or small compared to other errors or uncertainties. If they are large, and therefore contribute a lot to the spread in the readings and hence the standard deviation and standard error, then investing in better instrumentation may well be worth considering. If they are small, then you are stuck and the only way to improve the reliability of the mean is to increase the number of readings.

9.4 Deciding how many readings to take

Let us take the example of the bungee jump rope manufacturer again. The manufacturer has to take into account the fact that individual ropes will vary even when produced to the same specifications. This is because there will be small variations in thickness and composition which will result in slightly different stretchiness and hence differences in how far the bungee jumper will fall. You need to be sure that the ropes you are selling are safe. Here are the results for 100 jumps (using a dummy) for ropes, A, B and C. The lighter areas represent ±1SE (about 0.5 metres).

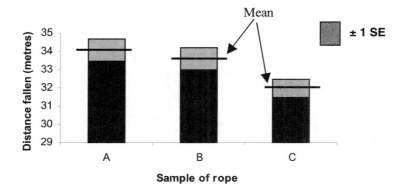

We can now say that ropes A and B will give about the same drop – the means are very similar and the SE is such that they 'overlap'. Rope C, by contrast, is very different. There is very little chance that the measurements for C are a fluke and that C is really the same as A and B. In fact, the chance is about one in a hundred (the mean is roughly three SEs away from that of B). So it would be sensible for the bungee rope manufacturer to sell ropes A and B as the same kind of rope. But s/he would be wise to sell C with separate specifications.

Here we have taken a sample of 100 – but why 100 rather than 50, or 500? This is where judgement comes in. Suppose the manufacturer decides that one particular specification of rope has to be the 'same' to within 2 per cent. In the above example, the SE was 0.5 metres in about 35 (see 'A' in the previous chart). This is less than the 2 per cent we need but only just. So a sample of 100 would be just adequate, but if the consequences of getting it wrong were great, then a wise person would do more to give a margin of error. An old engineers' rule is to work out how thick a beam needs to be (or whatever) and then double it!

9.5 Detecting patterns in data

Similarly we can show 'error bars' on line graphs as in the example below. Here we are looking at the distance fallen by 'bungee jumpers' of different mass. In this case we have used 3 standard errors to show the range of each measurement. This now tells us that the 'true value' is 99 per cent likely to be within the error bars for each value of mass. How many readings are necessary here? The example has enough in that it allows us to see the shape of the relationship clearly. But if the error bars were twice or three times that size, then it would be very much more difficult to be sure about the pattern. The sensible thing to do is gradually build up the number of readings, calculating SEs on the way, until the pattern becomes clear – it is a matter of judgement again.

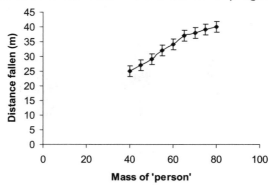

If you are still with us, you might want to turn to a statistics text book. You might begin by looking at 'linear regression' where the simple ideas discussed here are converted into the sort of statistics more commonly found in research literature.

9.6 Summary

In this chapter, we have considered the value of taking a large number of repeated measurements in giving us greater confidence in a measurement. Standard deviation and standard error can be used to describe the extent of the uncertainty of a measurement and to enable us to predict probability and risk. These statistics can also be used to explore the differences between the means of two or more sets of measurements and to check on patterns in data.

9.7 Looking forward, looking back

In looking forward we need to decide how many times to repeat a measurement or how big a sample to take to give reliable readings which will enable us to generalise from the results. In looking back, we can use the statistics discussed in this chapter to decide how much confidence can be placed in the results. Quantifying uncertainty in this way enables us to judge the reliability and validity of the data as a part of evidence.

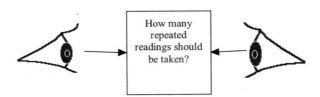

In considering the decision tree that follows, it is important to note again that it does not imply that decision-making is linear. If the statistics reveal that the sample size or the number of repeated readings is not going to result in the required reliability and validity then the investigator might choose to 'go back' and increase the sample size or the number of repeated readings.

Note also that all the decisions in the flowchart do not necessarily apply to a particular investigation. Some investigations will not require calculations of instrument error and some will not involve sampling. For example, many school chemistry and physics experiments do not involve issues to do with sampling.

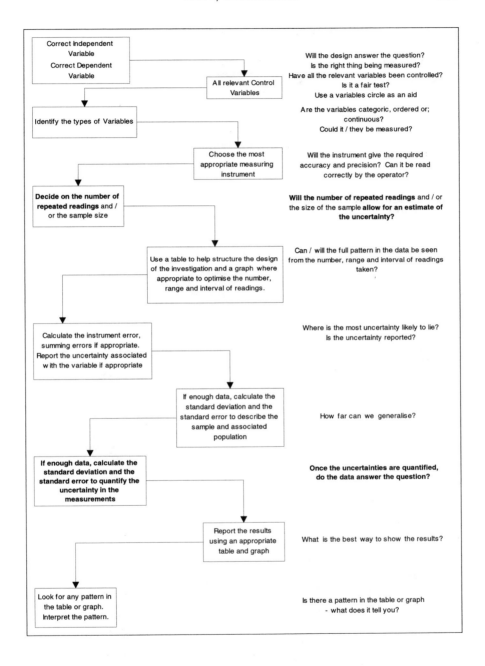

Correct Independent Variable
Correct Dependent Variable

Will the design answer the question?
Is the right thing being measured?
Have all the relevant variables been controlled?
Is it a fair test?
Use a variables circle as an aid

All relevant Control Variables

Identify the types of Variables

Are the variables categoric, ordered or;
continuous?
Could it / they be measured?

Choose the most appropriate measuring instrument

Will the instrument give the required accuracy and precision? Can it be read correctly by the operator?

Decide on the number of repeated readings and / or the sample size

Will the number of repeated readings and / or the size of the sample **allow for an estimate of the uncertainty?**

Use a table to help structure the design of the investigation and a graph where appropriate to optimise the number, range and interval of readings.

Can / will the full pattern in the data be seen from the number, range and interval of readings taken?

Calculate the instrument error, summing errors if appropriate. Report the uncertainty associated with the variable if appropriate

Where is the most uncertainty likely to lie?
Is the uncertainty reported?

If enough data, calculate the standard deviation and the standard error to describe the sample and associated population

How far can we generalise?

If enough data, calculate the standard deviation and the standard error to quantify the uncertainty in the measurements

Once the uncertainties are quantified, do the data answer the question?

Report the results using an appropriate table and graph

What is the best way to show the results?

Look for any pattern in the table or graph. Interpret the pattern.

Is there a pattern in the table or graph - what does it tell you?

Where are you?

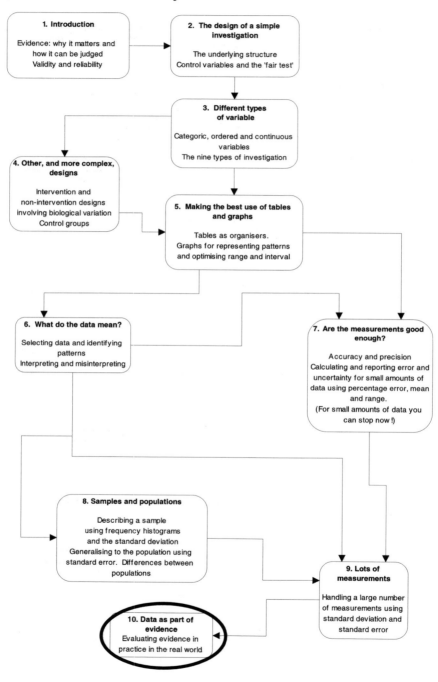

Chapter 10

Data as part of evidence

Introduction

> ## *Life-saving drug*
> ## *too expensive says*
> ## *health chief*

In all the last chapters, we have focused very deliberately on the scientific data itself. We can think of data as the heart of scientific evidence. But when we think about everyday issues which involve scientific evidence such as BSE (or bovine spongiform encephalitis), foot and mouth disease or vasectomy as a form of contraception, then there are other factors outside the data which also influence our opinion or decision. Being able to scrutinise the data and decide how good it is, is a very good starting point, but then we need to look more widely at other factors which contribute to evaluating the evidence as a whole.

In this final chapter we shall look, briefly, at some of the issues involved when real-life decisions have to be taken. The examples which follow are set in medical contexts and selected to illustrate just some of the issues that arise. We can only set the scene here but there are many books[1] and journals[2] to which the reader can turn to pursue the issues beyond the limits of this book.

---

[1] For example:
- The Royal Society (1997) Science, policy and risk (*Science in Society*, The Royal Society).
- Layton, D., Jenkins, E., MacGill, S., and Davey, A. (1993) Inarticulate science? Perspectives on the public understanding of science and some implications for science education (*Studies in Science Education*).
- Evans, G. and Durant, J. (1995) The relationship between knowledge and attitudes in the public understanding of science in Britain. *Public Understanding of Science* **4** 57–74.

[2] For example: Public Understanding of Science: an international journal of research in the public dimensions of science and technology (Institute of Physics).

10.1 A question of evidence

We shall begin by examining this question:

Does acupuncture 'work' for low back pain?

We shall draw heavily on a review by van Tulder and others[3]. Van Tulder and colleagues looked for all the evidence they could find on this issue in a review typical of attempts in the medical field to synthesise many studies and try to decide what, taken together, they mean in terms of treatment. They found a lot of individual studies which came to a range of conclusions about the effectiveness of acupuncture for low back pain. The aim of the review was to stand back and weigh up all the evidence by evaluating each study and then comparing the conclusions of the 'good' ones – the studies they thought reliable and valid. We shall use this example to illustrate how the ideas outlined in this book can be applied to 'everyday' issues like this.

To begin with, let us set the scene.

10.1.1 Background

Low back pain is a major health problem which causes disablement and absence from work. Although it can sometimes improve by itself over time, there are various treatments. But, as van Tulder writes, 'the effectiveness of most of these treatments has not been convincingly demonstrated'. As a result, medical treatment varies widely.

Acupuncture is a very old form of therapy with its roots in ancient Chinese philosophy. The theory is that all disorders are associated with specific points either on the skin surface or just below it. There are 361 classical acupuncture points and inserting a fine needle ('needling') at these points is believed to restore the balance in the body and relieve the disorder. Patients are usually advised to have a series of treatments maybe once or twice a week for several weeks to maximise the effect.

It is still not clear how acupuncture might work. There are various theories one of which is that acupuncture may stimulate the production of substances within the central nervous system which act as pain relievers.

But does acupuncture really work – how can we find out? What is the evidence?

[3] Tulder, M. W. van, Cherkin, D. C., Berman, B., Lao, L., and Koes, B. W. Acupuncture for low back pain (Cochrane Review), in *Cochrane Library Issue 2* (2001) Oxford: Update Software.

10.1.2 The structure of the studies

Let us think a moment about what the structure of an investigation into 'Does acupuncture "work" for low back pain?' would look like. A circle of variables will help to clarify some of the relevant variables:

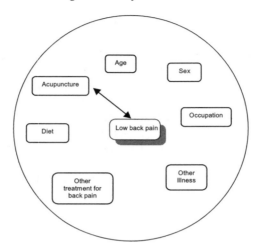

The independent variable is the acupuncture treatment, or lack of it, and the dependent variable is low back pain. Let us look more closely at these two variables:

The independent variable

The treatment is the independent variable but we need more than one value. To find out whether acupuncture 'works', we need to compare treatment by acupuncture with either some other treatment or no treatment at all.

These are the comparisons that van Tulder and his associates found in the studies they looked at:

1. Acupuncture compared to no treatment, or, in some studies, acupuncture plus basic drug treatment (e.g. pain killers) compared to basic drug treatment without acupuncture.
2. Acupuncture compared to 'placebo' or 'sham' treatment:
   (a) Placebo treatment: treatment in which the needles are attached to the skin surface but do not go into the skin.
   (b) Sham treatment: treatment in which the needles prick the skin surface but are placed in an area close to, but not in, the acupuncture points.
3. Acupuncture compared to conventional treatment.

Notice that in all of these cases the independent variable has only two values and is *categoric*. For example, in the first comparison, the two values are 'acupuncture' or 'no acupuncture'.

The dependent variable

How can the dependent variable, low back pain, be defined? Van Tulder and colleagues found several different measurements of back pain in the studies they looked at. Here are three examples:

- a measurement of the intensity of the pain;
- a measure of physical movement such as degree of straight leg raising or spinal flexibility;
- the number of days off work.

Are the measurements good enough (valid and reliable)?

The first measure, the measurement of pain intensity, is problematic because subjective or self-report measures are inherently unreliable. One way of measuring pain is to ask the patient to rate the pain using words such as 'none', 'mild', 'moderate' and 'severe': so it is an ordered variable. This can either be done in relation to the pain as a whole or in relation to descriptive words such as 'throbbing', 'stabbing', 'aching', etc. An alternative way, which is widely used and which was the method used in the RCTs (randomised controlled trials) that van Tulder examined, is to use a 'visual analogue scale' or VAS. This method presents the patient with a line 10cm long. The patient is told that one end of the line represents no pain and the other end represents the worst pain imaginable. The patient is then asked to make a mark on the line showing the intensity of his or her pain. This mark is then measured with a ruler to get a numerical measure of pain intensity. The advantage of this method over the other descriptive measures is that the measurement of pain becomes a continuous variable. Studies have been done to demonstrate that VAS is at least as good as the verbal rating scales but its validity is still questioned[4] not least because there remains an element of subjectivity.

The second measure, measures of physical movement, is likely to be more straightforward in that there can be little dispute about the angle to which a patient can raise each leg from a lying position, providing the measurement method is standardised. So this is clearly a continuous variable. It is more reliable, but is it a valid measure of pain? We can all think of instances where you act *despite* pain.

We might question whether the third measure, the number of days off work, is a valid measure. There are people who take more time off

---

[4] Carlsson, A. M. (1983) 'Assessment of chronic pain I. Aspects of the reliability and validity of the visual analogue scale', *Pain,* 16: 87–101.

work than is justified and, conversely, people who continue to work despite considerable pain (depending on their occupation of course). Nevertheless, if the sample is large enough, it may be a 'good enough' measure, provided that the will to work is randomly distributed – that there are as many who shirk as there are those who martyr themselves!

Consider again our 9 'types': the combinations of types of independent and dependent variables (see Chapter 3, pages 35–42). Where do the acupuncture experiments lie?

	Dependent variable		
Independent variable	Categoric	Ordered	Continuous
Categoric	1	2	3
Ordered	4	5	6
Continuous	7	8	9

Knowing that the independent variable is categoric, then we are looking at the first horizontal row only (shaded). The three measures of the dependent variable aim to make the measurement of 'pain' a numerical value and preferably a continuous variable. The three examples quoted above would put the investigations into type 3 in the table.

Remember that we discussed earlier in the book how continuous variables provide stronger and more useful data than categoric variables. So, in our acupuncture example, instead of reporting that a person did or did not have lower back pain after acupuncture treatment, it is more useful and more believable to be able to say that the pain decreased by a stated 'amount' or that you are likely to have X per cent more flexibility in your spine after acupuncture. That will also enable comparisons of different treatments. For example does another treatment, e.g. osteopathy (manipulation of the bones), usually help relieve pain as much as, or less, or more, than acupuncture? Provided the investigators measure pain intensity in the same way, then we could compare the effect of such treatments.

Control variables

What can be done about all the control variables, some of which we have identified in the circle of variables? We can use a control group and randomly allocate patients to either the experimental group (treated with acupuncture) or the control group (no treatment, placebo or sham treatment or conventional treatment). That way with a big enough sample we could randomise control variables like age, sex, occupation, etc. – there will be as many old as young in the treatment and non-treatment group so they will effectively 'cancel each other out' in terms of their effects. Van Tulder and colleagues decided to include only this type of study (RCTs) and exclude studies where patients were not randomised.

The sample

All the patients in the samples suffered from 'non-specific' (without an obvious cause) low back pain. Van Tulder excluded studies which included patients with specific conditions likely to cause back pain such as some types of cancer, osteoporosis or arthritis. In effect, then, the review controlled for cause of back pain (actually to 'unknown cause'!) by *selection* of those eligible to be included in the sample.

10.1.3 Validity of the design

Van Tulder and colleagues used a recognised list of 10 criteria to assess the quality or validity of the design of the studies. Here are three examples of the 10 criteria by way of illustration:

1. Was the method of randomisation described and adequate?
2. Was the withdrawal/drop-out rate unlikely to cause bias?
3. Was the timing of the outcome assessment in both groups comparable?

If the answer to more than five of these 10 criteria is 'yes', then the study is judged to be of higher quality. These criteria are factors which can affect the validity of the outcomes of a study. For example, in relation to the second criterion, supposing the study was comparing acupuncture with no treatment and a lot of patients from the control group dropped out of the study during the treatment period. There might be something significant about the drop-outs. For example, their backs might have got better by themselves while the remaining patients in the control group still had severe back pain. This could bias the results in favour of acupuncture.

Similarly the third criterion, the timing of the assessment of the outcomes, could affect validity. This is a control variable: the follow-up time should be kept the same. If patients were followed up for three months after treatment in the acupuncture group compared to only one month in the control group, again some of the patients might improve considerably by themselves after three months.

10.1.4 The data

Here is an example of the data for the studies. The figures show measures of low back pain in the experimental (acupuncture) and control group (no treatment) in two studies when patients were asked about their back pain shortly after treatment/no treatment.

	Experimental group		Control group	
	Group size	Mean (SD)	Group size	Mean (SD)
Study 1	23	2.7 (n.r)	16	4.7 (n.r)
Study 2	30	4 (5)	10	6.1 (1.75)

n.r = not reported

Since the mean values for pain are lower in the experimental group (those receiving acupuncture) than in the control group (2.7 compared to 4.7 and 4 compared to 6.1), then, at first sight, it looks as if acupuncture results in the reduction of lower back pain. But let us take a closer look.

First, we should note that the sample sizes are not large. The control group in study 2 has only 10 patients. We might want to be cautious about the results in the light of this.

Secondly, in Chapter 8, we noted that the standard deviation is a much better measure of the shape of the data than the mean alone (see Chapter 8, pages 143–145). Let us remind ourselves of what that means in relation to this example. Suppose you have low back pain and you want to know whether you are likely to benefit from acupuncture treatment. The mean tells you the average reduction in pain but it does not tell you whether most people benefited about this much or whether some benefited a lot, others very little and quite a lot did not benefit much at all. The mean does not tell you how the data are distributed. So we need to look at the standard deviation because this can tell us, for example, how much pain relief two-thirds of the sample obtained. Notice that the standard deviation is not reported in the first study so we can go no further.

But the SDs are reported in the second study. Notice that, for the experimental group, the standard deviation is 5 which seems relatively high given that the mean is 4. Assuming a normal distribution, we can use the SD as follows.

Experimental group:
Mean = 4 ± 5. So, two-thirds of the patients after acupuncture treatment had pain levels of between −1 and +9 (−1 is actually off the scale altogether).

Control group:

Mean = 6.1 ± 1.75. So, two-thirds of the patients in the control group had pain levels of between 4.35 and 7.85. Notice that, because the SD was high in the experimental group, the spread of the data in the group was wide (that is what the SD measures). This means that acupuncture treatment might give you excellent relief (–1) but it might not (+9, which is worse than any of the control group). There is also considerable overlap between the two groups which could indicate that having the treatment or not will not make much difference to some low back pain sufferers.

You may remember that in Chapter 8 we noted that standard-deviation describes the distribution of the sample but that the standard error (or SE) tells us about the sample mean in relation to the mean of the whole population. It is a measure of how typical the sample is. We know that calculating the standard error (or indeed the standard deviation) is of doubtful value when the sample size is as low as 10, but let us do it and see whether it confirms our suspicion that the data are not very robust.

Since we know the standard deviation and the sample size for study 2, we can work out the SE as follows:

$$SE = \frac{s}{\sqrt{n}}$$

So for our example:

For experimental group:

$$SE = \frac{5}{\sqrt{30}} = 0.91$$

For control group:

$$SE = \frac{1.75}{\sqrt{10}} = 0.55$$

What does this tell us?

It tells us that the mean for the population (all such sufferers who fit the selection criteria for the sample in the first place) is 68 per cent likely to be within the range 3.1–4.9 for the experimental group (mean ± 1SE) and 5.5–6.6 for the control group.

If we want to be 95 per cent sure about the population means, we would have to go to ±2SE, and the values then will lie in the range 2.2–5.8 for the experimental group and 5 and 7.2 for the control group.

Let us plot these figures on a bar chart which will help us to see what this means more clearly:

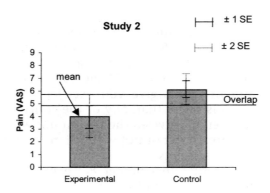

We can see that there is no overlap between the experimental and control groups if we look at the mean plus or minus 1 standard error – that is, the two groups appear to have different levels of pain. So the patients who have had acupuncture seem to be faring better. What the SE tells us that there is a two in three chance that the population from which these samples were drawn would benefit from acupuncture.

But when we look at ±2SE, there *is* an overlap as indicated on the chart. This means that there is *not* a 19 in 20 chance that the population from which these samples were drawn would benefit from acupuncture. So the odds of acupuncture working, based on this evidence alone, are between two in three (± 1SE) and 19 in 20 (± 2SE), but no better than that. You may think that this is good enough to give it a try. In this case, where there is unlikely to be any side effects other than to your wallet, this may well be true. But if there were serious side effects, or the cost of the treatment were very high, then other factors come into play and the treatment might then be judged simply not worth while at those odds.

Van Tulder and his colleagues looked carefully at the data in this study and in all the other studies. The reviewers were not told the authors' names, their institution (e.g. hospital or clinic etc.) or the journal in which the study was published. If they had been allowed to see any of this information, it might have biased the reviewers' opinions.

Taking into account the data, the method and the sample size, the reviewers rated the findings as one of the following:

- positive (i.e. showed acupuncture was effective);
- neutral (showed little difference between the two groups);
- negative (i.e. showed acupuncture was ineffective);
- unclear.

Below are the summaries of the two studies considered above taken from van Tulder's review. In the 'Notes' column, the authors' conclusions and the reviewers' ratings are compared. It is interesting to note how frequently van Tulder comes to a more pessimistic view of the results than do the original authors. It is very difficult to be objective when you have just spent a great deal of time and effort carrying out research into a subject which may be very dear to your heart!

Study	Methods	Participants	Interventions	Outcomes	Notes
Study 1	RCT; randomisation was carried out by having prepared in advance a small box with 50 identically-sized pieces of paper, folded so that they could not be read. 25 had A and 25 had B written on them. The box was shaken and one of the pieces of paper was removed from the box blindly.	50 patients recruited via newspapers. Inclusion criteria: Low back pain for 6 months or more, no previous acupuncture treatments, no history of diabetes, infection or cancer, and not more than 2 back surgeries.	Acupuncture:10 or more treatments, approximately 10 weeks. Control: patients on the waiting list: no treatment.	Results after 10 weeks in acupuncture and after 15 weeks in control group: reduction in pain score (11-point scale): acupuncture group 51% versus control group 2%. Inadequate treatment in 11 of the 50 patients treated with acupuncture.	Conclusion of authors 'positive'; conclusion of reviewers 'unclear'. Large number of drop-outs. Difference in follow-up time.
Study 2	Randomisation procedure not described.	43 patients from 2 clinics. Inclusion criteria: Low back pain for 6 months or more, no previous surgery.	Acupuncture: 10 sessions of 30 mins. Control: patients on the waiting list: no treatment.	Results: Improvements on various scales in acupuncture group after 6 weeks and after 6 months.	Conclusion of authors for pain 'positive'; conclusion of reviewers 'positive'.

Study 2 was rated as positive by the reviewers. Do you agree? How positive would you be prepared to be?

10.1.5 Comparisons with other data and generalisability

Let us now return to our question:

Does acupuncture work for low back pain?

You might think that as a single study, study 2 is not very convincing and, in the light of the small sample size and the overlap between the two groups, it is wise to be cautious.

But the point of van Tulder's review is to look at *all* the relevant studies. It might well be that a lot of studies have come up with the same rather doubtful result. If they all point in the same direction, then even though each of them might, on its own, not be convincing and the reliability and validity of some aspects of the studies may be in question, the fact that all of them point in the same direction may give you more confidence in the data. This is where judgement comes in. But if half the studies point one way, and half point the other, then we can conclude that the results of each study are themselves randomly distributed about zero, indicating that current evidence suggests that acupuncture does no good at all.

Van Tulder and his colleagues examined each individual study in detail using the same criteria to report on the validity of the design and scrutinising the data to rate the findings. Then they looked at all the studies that had focused on the same independent variable (e.g. acupuncture compared to conventional treatment) and arrived at a 'level' of evidence. They define four levels of evidence:

Level 1: Strong evidence – provided by generally consistent findings in multiple higher quality RCTs.
Level 2: Moderate evidence – provided by generally consistent findings in one higher quality RCT and one or more lower quality RCTs.
Level 3: Limited evidence – provided by generally consistent findings in one or more lower quality RCTs.
Level 4: No evidence – if there were no RCTs or if the results were conflicting.

The studies were considered to be conflicting if less than one-third were either positive or negative for a specific measure (e.g. pain, days off work, etc.).

These levels of evidence are not universal and van Tulder advises readers to apply their own rating system to see if the conclusions change 'because there is no consensus yet on how to assess the strength of the evidence'. Nevertheless the process of evaluating the evidence is described in enough detail so that the reader can decide whether or not s/he agrees with the criteria.

Here are the conclusions of van Tulder's review:

1. Acupuncture compared to no treatment.

Evidence? Level 4: No evidence that acupuncture is more effective than no treatment.

2. Acupuncture compared to placebo or 'sham' treatment.

Evidence? Level 3: There was limited evidence that acupuncture is *not* more effective than placebo or sham treatment for low back pain.

3. Acupuncture compared to conventional treatment.

Evidence? Level 2: There was moderate evidence that acupuncture is *not* more effective than a specified conventional treatment.

By looking at all the relevant studies, we can also say something about the *generalisability* of the results and the pattern in the data. Generalisability, in this example, means how far can we apply the results to the general population of low back pain sufferers? Reviews of this kind, which examine the sampling process in each study very carefully and then compare the results of different studies, enable us to answer this question. In this review, random samples of back pain sufferers were used in the studies but patients who had specific conditions which was likely to cause back pain were excluded. So van Tulder's conclusions (above) apply only to people who suffer from 'non-specific' low back pain. So we can generalise as far as that.

10.2 Circles of evidence

In the acupuncture example we saw how data from individual experiments was:

- Examined internally, so to speak, for its quality and therefore its reliability and validity (how much weight can be placed on the data and do they answer the question);
- Compared to other studies to see if, together, they are more convincing than one study alone, or whether they are in conflict and to see how far we can generalise from the results.

But we have not yet looked very far out into the real world represented by the outer circle in the diagram below.[5]

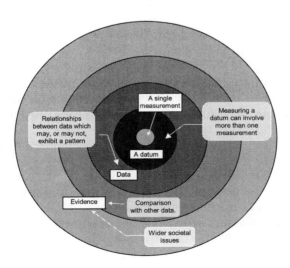

---

[5] The website, http://www.dur.ac.uk/~dd0www/evidence_main1.htm, gives a detailed description of each circle of evidence in the diagram

10.3 The 'real world' – wider societal issues

What are these 'wider societal issues'? Consider first the role of evidence-based medicine.

10.3.1 Data, costs and values in evidence-based medicine

In medicine wherever it is possible, thorough reviews of treatments (like the acupuncture example above) are carried out to determine the strength of the currently available evidence. Data from different sources are compared. But how are these ideas applied in practice when the patient sees the doctor at the surgery? At this point, a whole host of other factors come into play.

Suppose the review is about the effectiveness of a drug. The patient in the doctor's surgery may be interested to hear about the evidence of a drug's effectiveness, but they might also want to know about its side effects and its consequences for their lifestyle. For example, suppose the patient is a long distance truck driver but the drug tends to make you drowsy and it is recommended that you do not drive while taking it. The truck driver might decide

- not to take the drug rather than forfeit his/her livelihood;
- s/he might, on the advice of the doctor, opt for an alternative less effective drug which has different side effects;
- decide to take the drug and adjust his/her lifestyle.

So, the implications of the evidence have to be looked at for the individual patient. In this particular case, considerations of the side effects were as important as the data about the effectiveness of the drug for the patient in arriving at a decision.

From the doctor's point of view, a particular drug might be very effective but it might also be very expensive. If there are a significant number of patients in the practice who, on clinical grounds alone, will be eligible for the drug, the doctor might opt for a cheaper slightly less effective drug. So, here, cost is the deciding factor.

Many health-care decisions are taken at the population level, that is, the promotion of the health of the population as a whole. This is particularly clear in vaccination programmes. The evidence is that vaccination is effective for the population as a whole but it is also recognised that a minority of children may suffer damage. Mass vaccination programmes are carried out 'for the good of the population'. You could argue that in this case the population is valued more highly than the individual. So vaccination is based on evidence but it is also based on society's values, as reflected by the government through the health authority.

Muir Gray[6] identifies three factors which interact in evidence-based decision making for populations – the data, values and resources, as shown in the following diagram:

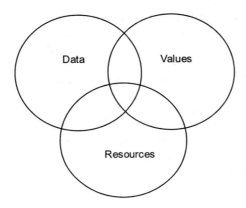

Source: adapted from Muir Gray (2001)

Muir Gray suggests that the final decision may be driven by any or all of these three factors.

Values such as ageism (valuing young or middle-aged people more than older people) have been known to drive evidence-based decisions. We can think of this issue in relation to policy on heart or kidney transplants or in relation to breast screening both of which have been the subject of criticism. When resources are scarce, then hard decisions based on the data, but in some cases ultimately driven by a society's predominant value systems, may have to be taken.

10.3.2 Bias

Bias takes many forms. It can be intricately tied to prejudice, preconceptions, fear, authority, status and the notion of 'interested' parties. All of these can mean that there is a risk of the evaluation of evidence being 'coloured' or swayed in one direction or another and more than the evidence alone warrants.

We noted in the acupuncture example that the reviewers were not told the names of the authors of the studies, their place of employment or the name of the publication. This was because, for example,

6 Muir Gray, J. A. (2001) 'Using systematic reviews for evidence-based policy making', in *Systematic Reviews of Healthcare: Meta-Analysis in Context* 2nd edition, BMJ Books.

if the reviewer had personally known the author (in a positive or a negative way), it might have influenced how the data were judged. Similarly, if a reviewer had strong *preconceptions* about alternative medicine in one direction or another then his/her final judgement might have been influenced.

The issue of *status* and *authority* is also a difficult one. If a well-established and highly-regarded scientist publishes in a well-respected journal, it tends to be more difficult to reject the findings than if the study had come from a less well-known source.

The notion of *interested parties* is often associated with the source of funding of a study. So, for example, if a drug company funds research into the effects of a new drug, we might choose to examine the findings very carefully knowing that the drug company wants to promote its products in a positive way. This is the reason for many scientific journals asking authors to declare any 'conflict of interest' and to state how the research was funded.

10.4 What if there is no evidence?

What if there are no valid and reliable data? Then the centre of our circles of evidence will be missing. In that case, the next best thing, and indeed the only option, is to resort to the outer layers of the circles of evidence. We then arrive at a decision based on other factors such as values, common sense, experience or 'consensus'. 'Consensus' is the term applied to medical decision making when there is no hard evidence and a team of experts makes recommendations based on the opinion of the majority.

10.5 Summary

In this final chapter, we have tried to show that data lies at the heart of evidence but that there are other 'layers' of evidence which also need to be taken into consideration and that can be just as influential.

To make decisions based on evidence, we need to:

- examine the data for validity and reliability;
- search for any other data to support or refute the conclusions of an individual study;
- look at the wider issues which are relevant to the final decision and which might influence the interpretation of the data.

We have seen, illustrated by the van Tulder review, the process of peer review of scientific evidence in action. Each experimental study is scrutinised for its design, the reliability of the measurements, the validity of the sample and the quality of the resulting data and its interpretation. It is not a clear-cut exercise as science is often represented. It involves critical analysis and judgement.

What we hope to have provided in this book is a tool kit of ideas that will help in informing that judgement.

10.6 Looking forward, looking back

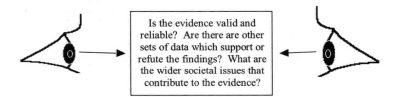

Is the evidence valid and reliable? Are there are other sets of data which support or refute the findings? What are the wider societal issues that contribute to the evidence?

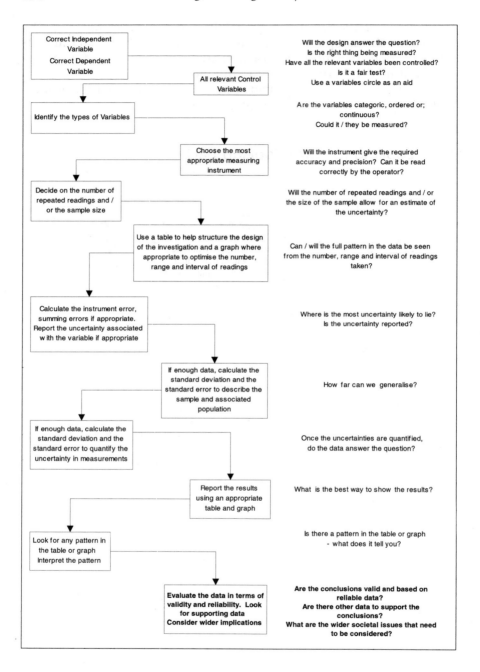

Correct Independent Variable
Correct Dependent Variable

All relevant Control Variables

Will the design answer the question?
Is the right thing being measured?
Have all the relevant variables been controlled?
Is it a fair test?
Use a variables circle as an aid

Identify the types of Variables

Are the variables categoric, ordered or; continuous?
Could it / they be measured?

Choose the most appropriate measuring instrument

Will the instrument give the required accuracy and precision? Can it be read correctly by the operator?

Decide on the number of repeated readings and / or the sample size

Will the number of repeated readings and / or the size of the sample allow for an estimate of the uncertainty?

Use a table to help structure the design of the investigation and a graph where appropriate to optimise the number, range and interval of readings

Can / will the full pattern in the data be seen from the number, range and interval of readings taken?

Calculate the instrument error, summing errors if appropriate. Report the uncertainty associated with the variable if appropriate

Where is the most uncertainty likely to lie?
Is the uncertainty reported?

If enough data, calculate the standard deviation and the standard error to describe the sample and associated population

How far can we generalise?

If enough data, calculate the standard deviation and the standard error to quantify the uncertainty in measurements

Once the uncertainties are quantified, do the data answer the question?

Report the results using an appropriate table and graph

What is the best way to show the results?

Look for any pattern in the table or graph Interpret the pattern

Is there a pattern in the table or graph - what does it tell you?

Evaluate the data in terms of validity and reliability. Look for supporting data Consider wider implications

Are the conclusions valid and based on reliable data?
Are there other data to support the conclusions?
What are the wider societal issues that need to be considered?

Index